CHURCHES

A photo book by
Stev Peter

The True Church can never fail

"I like the silence of a church, before the service begins better than any preaching."
Ralph Waldo Emerson

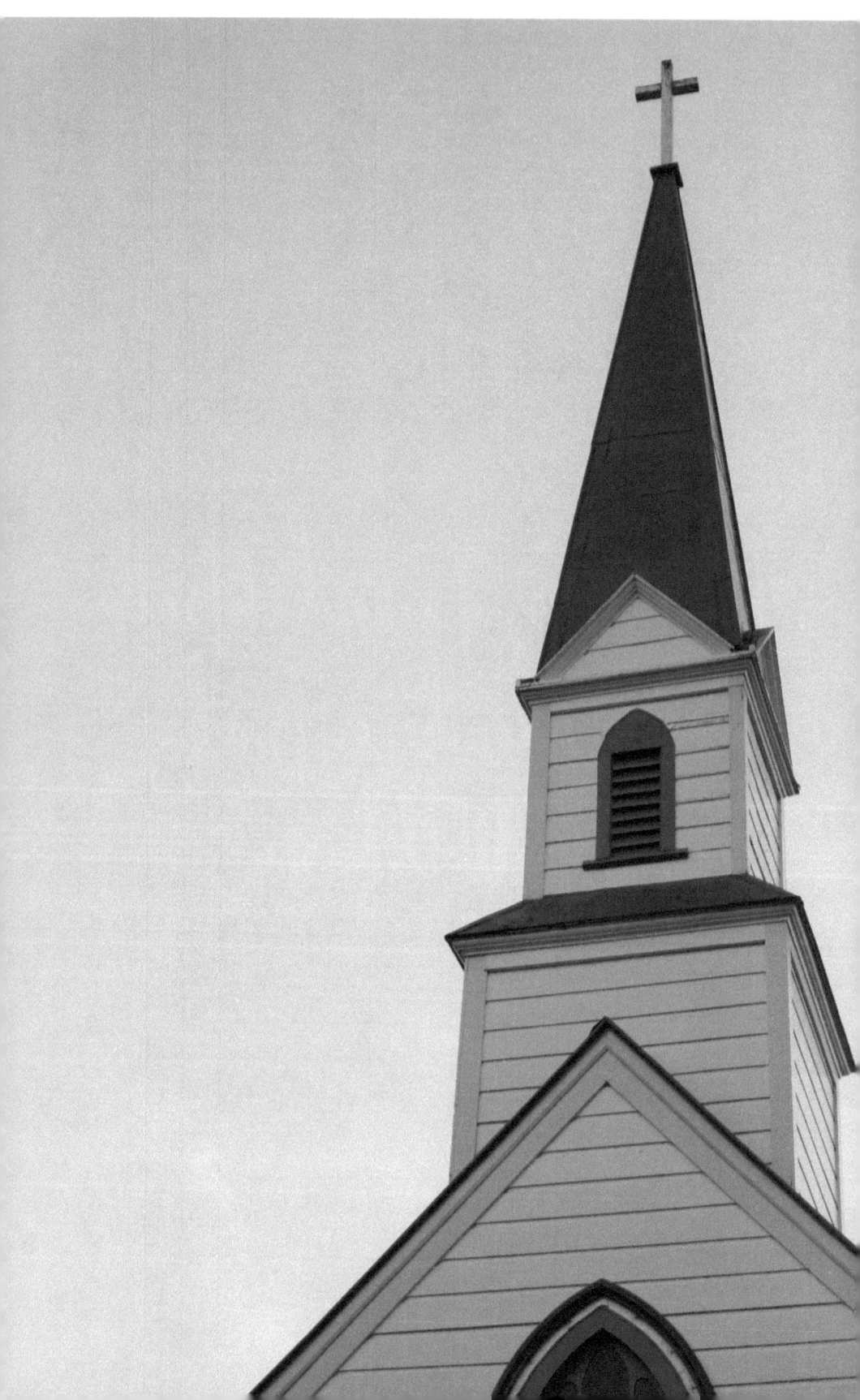

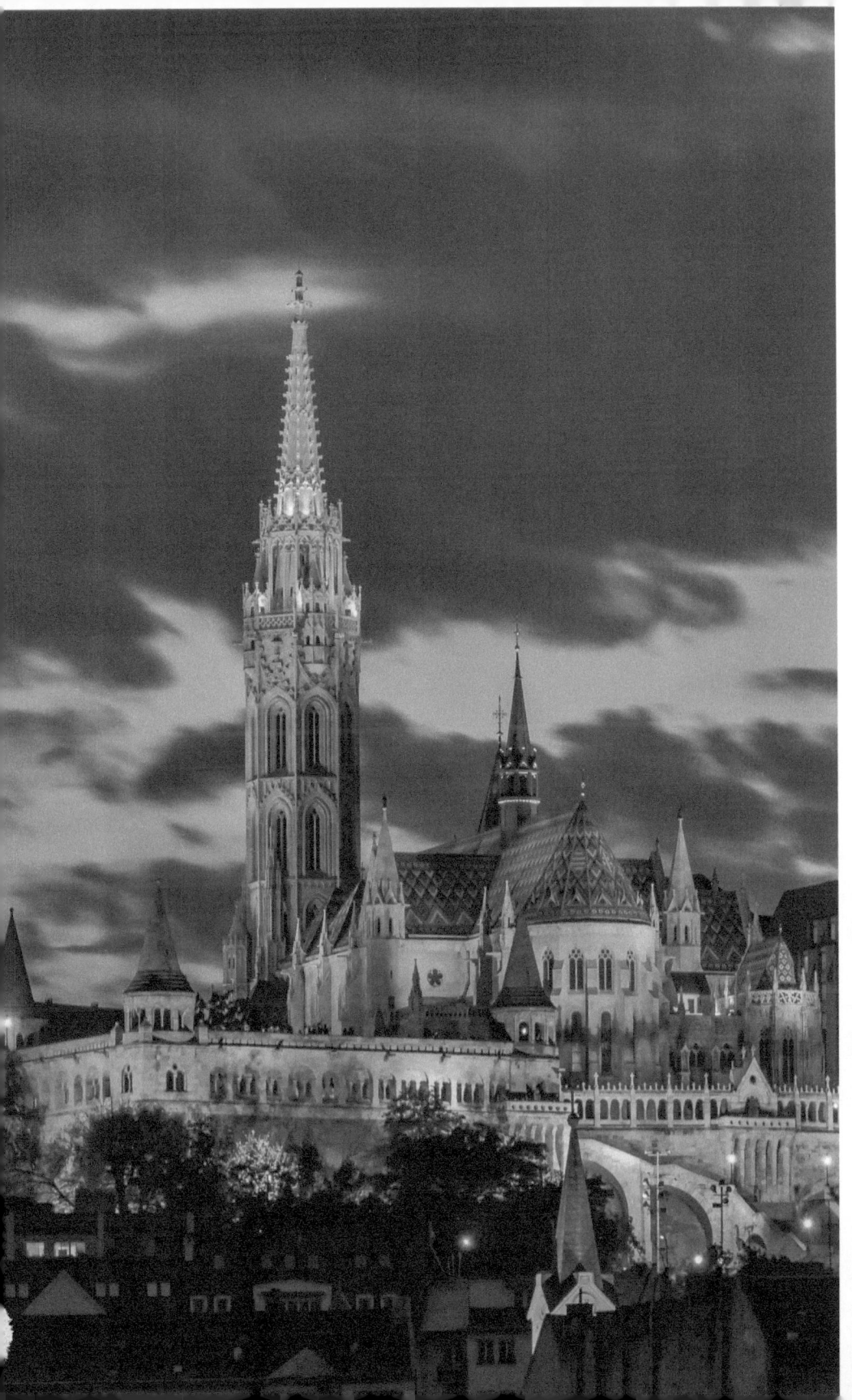

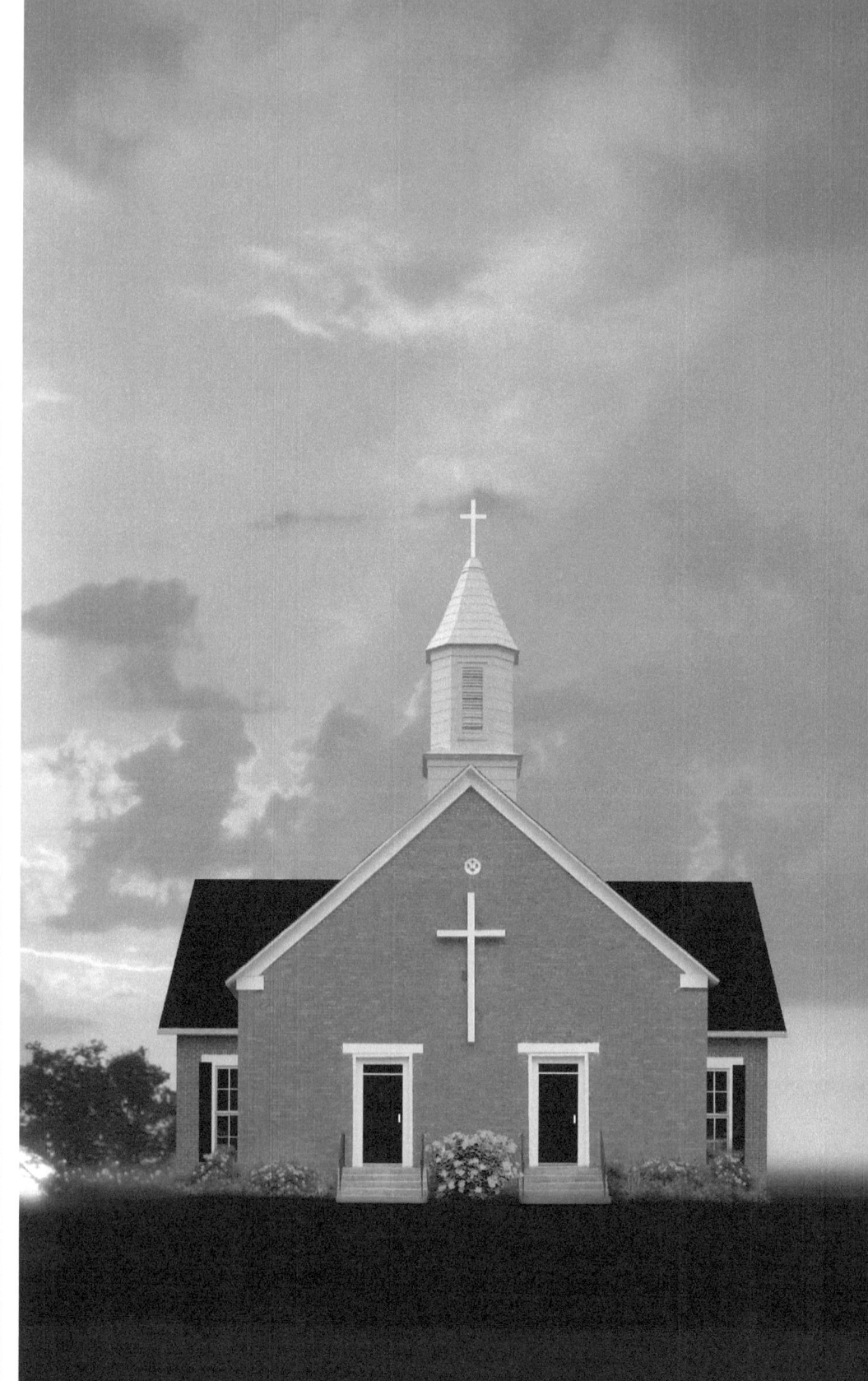

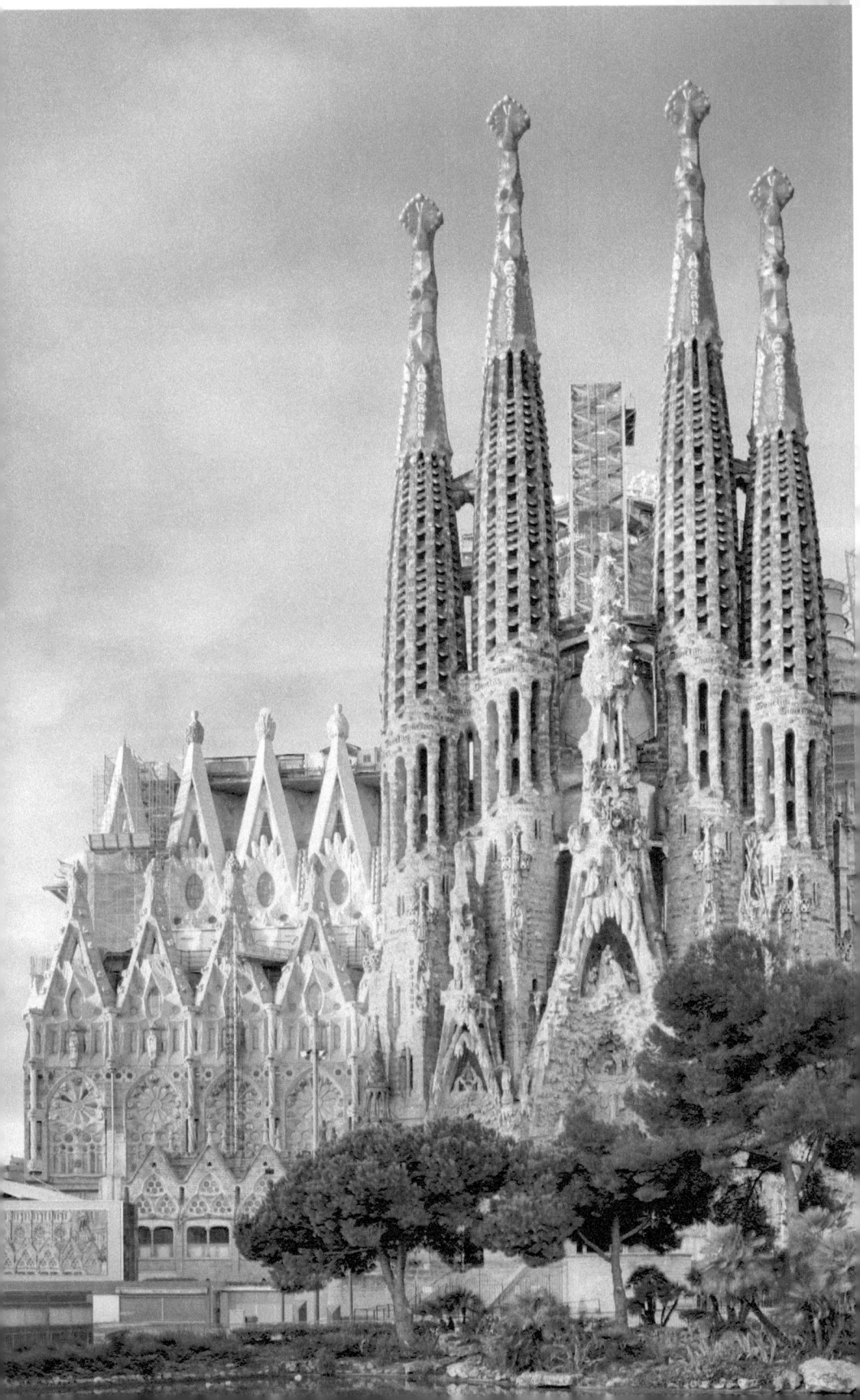

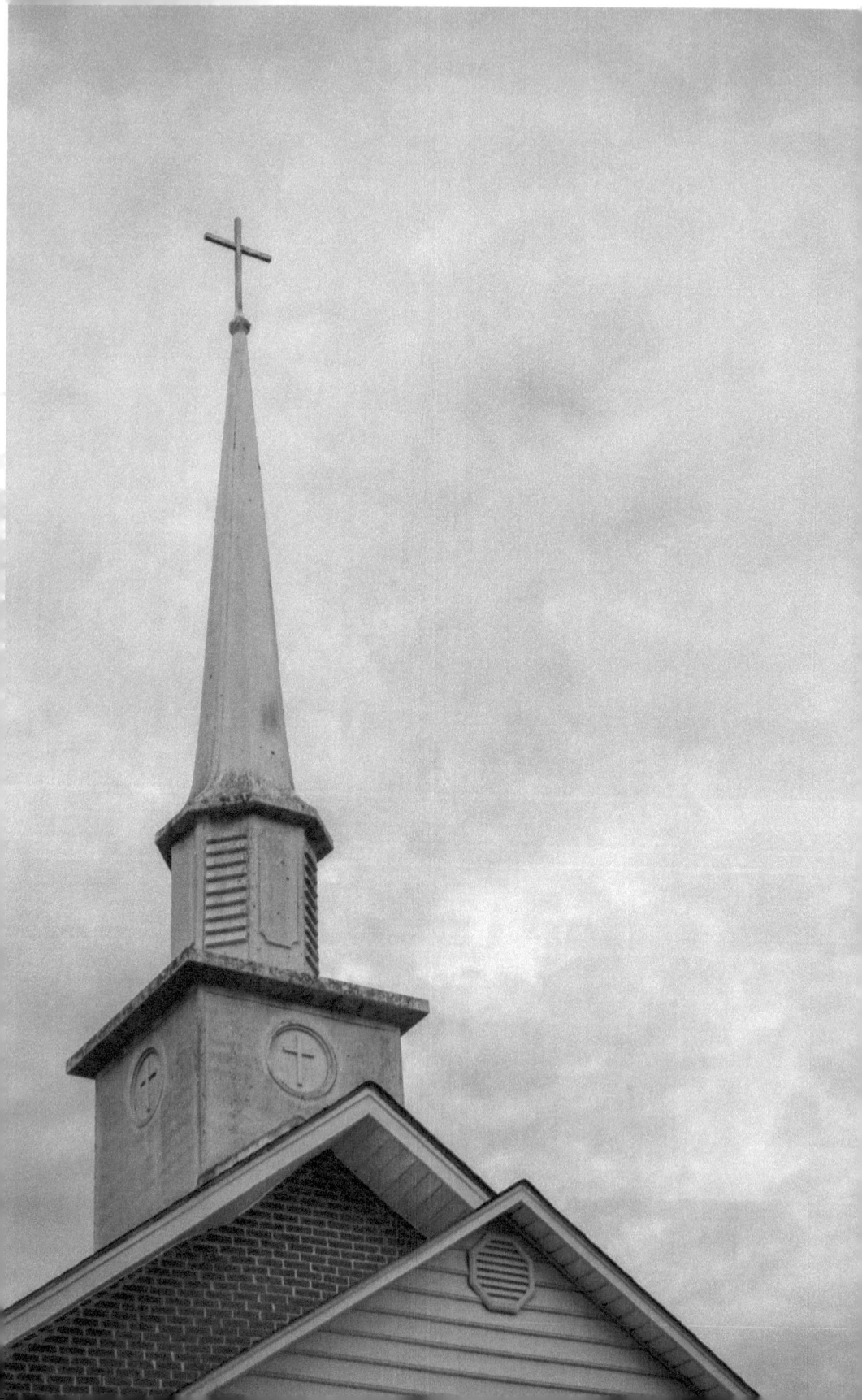

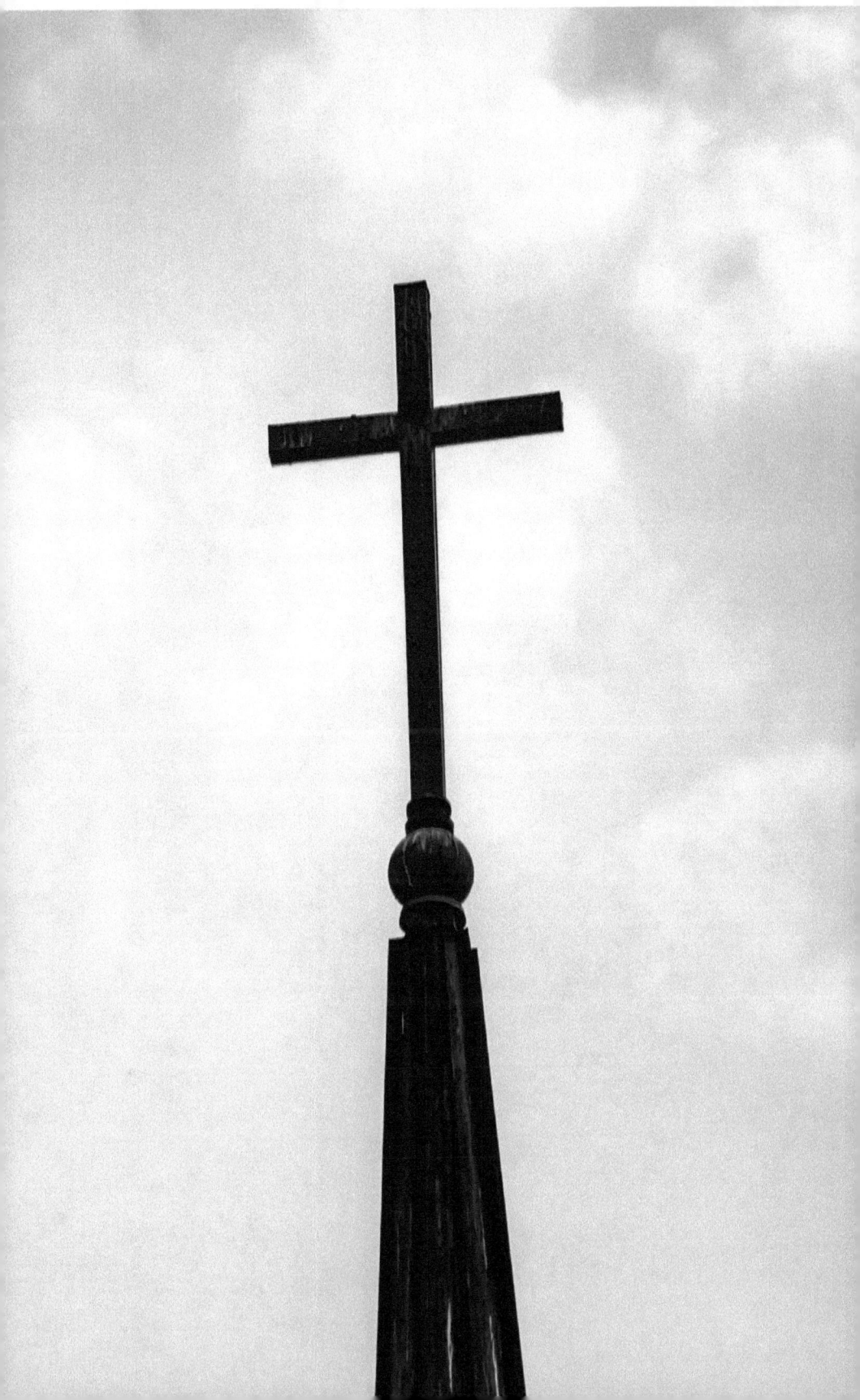

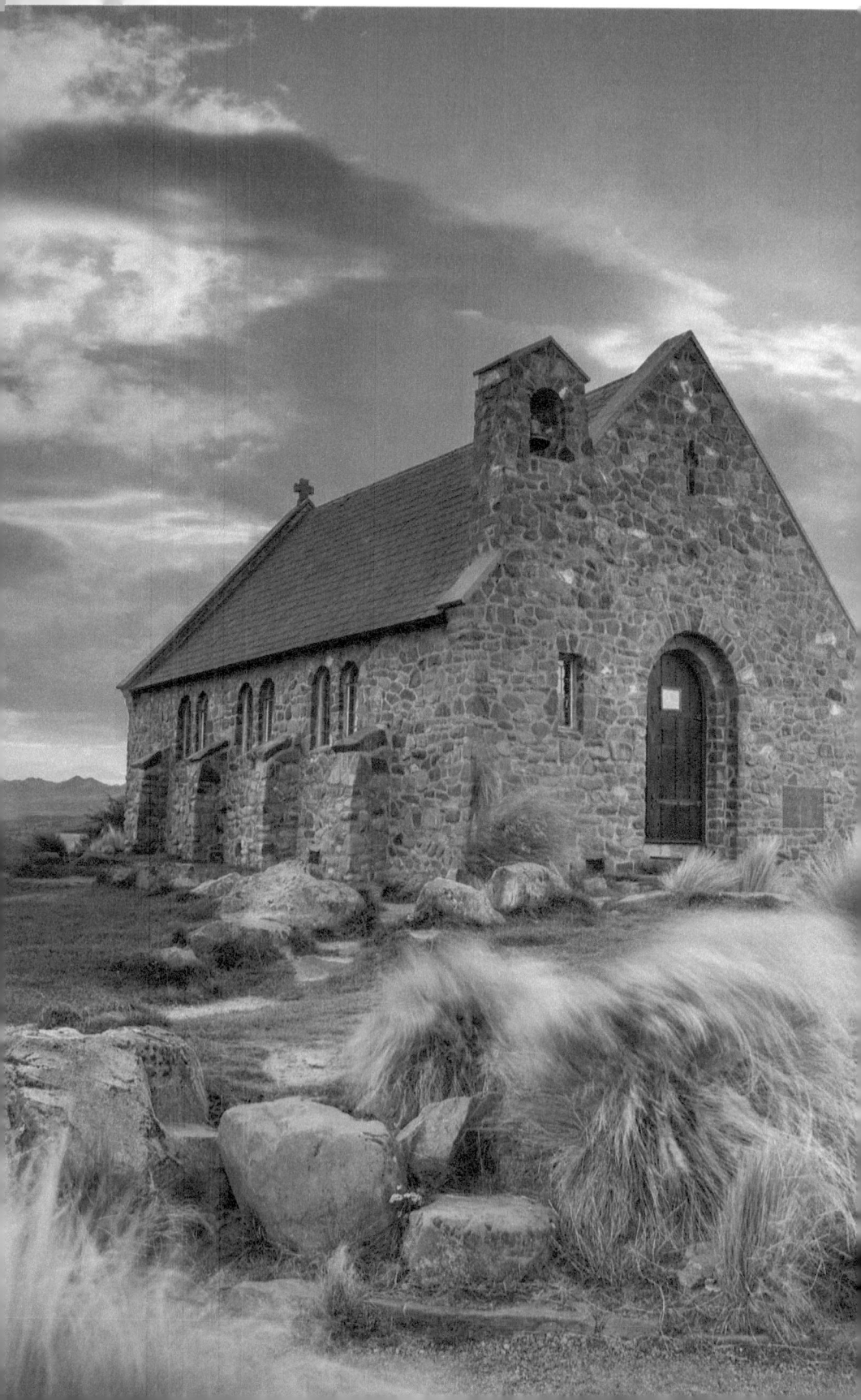

"In the Church, considered as a social organism, the mysteries inevitably degenerate into beliefs."
Simone Weil

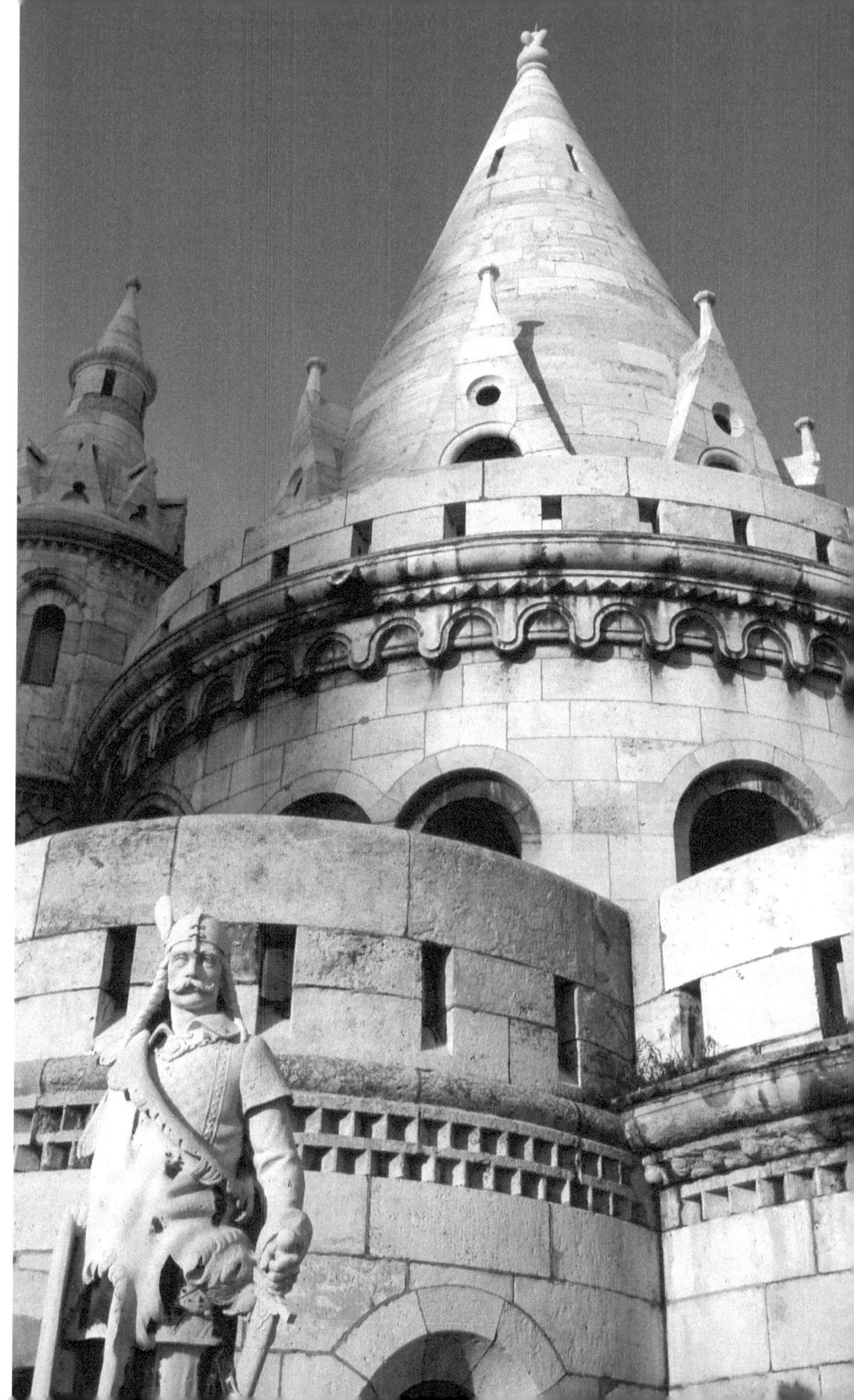

"The Church is the one institution that exists for those outside it."
William Tyndale

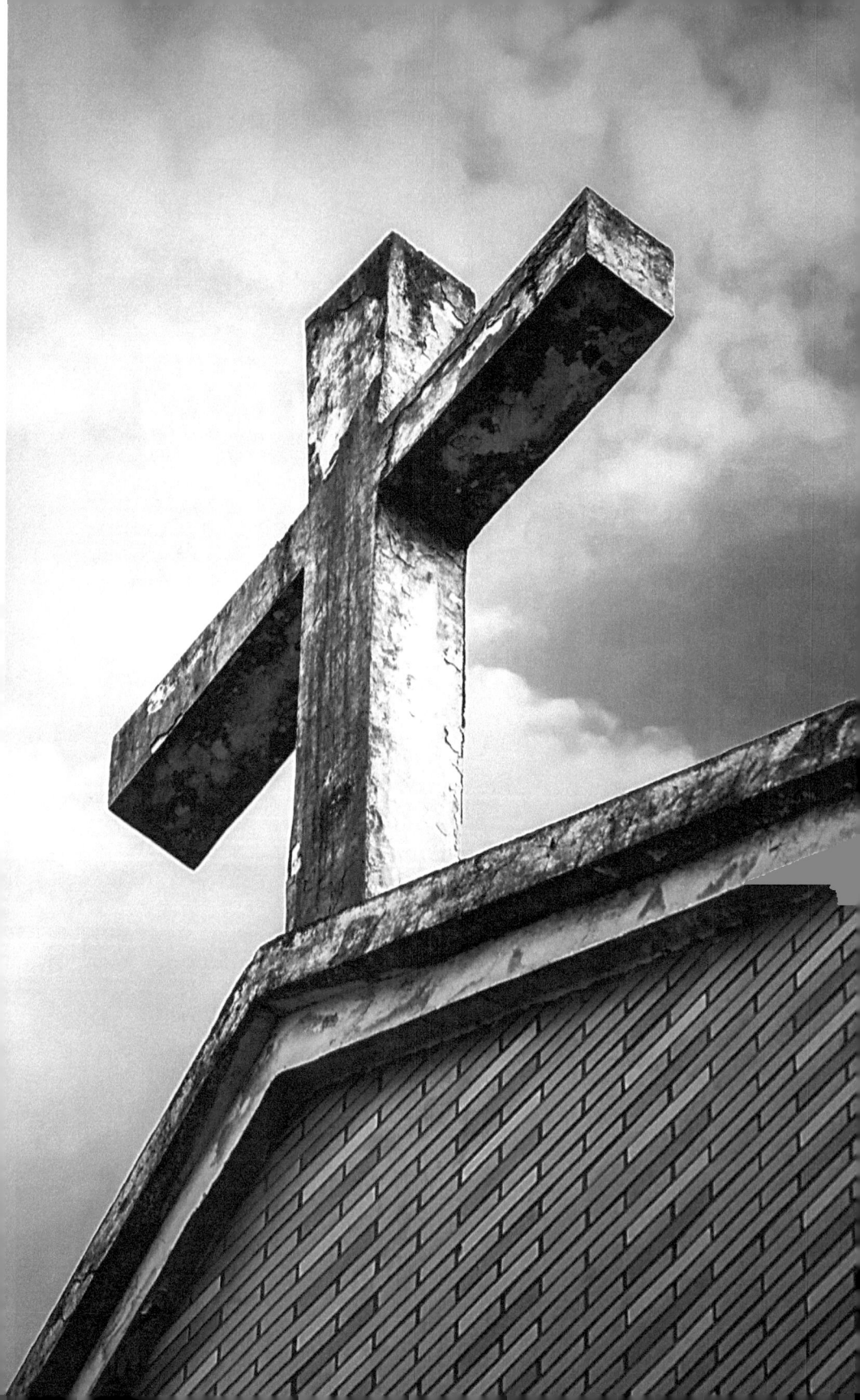

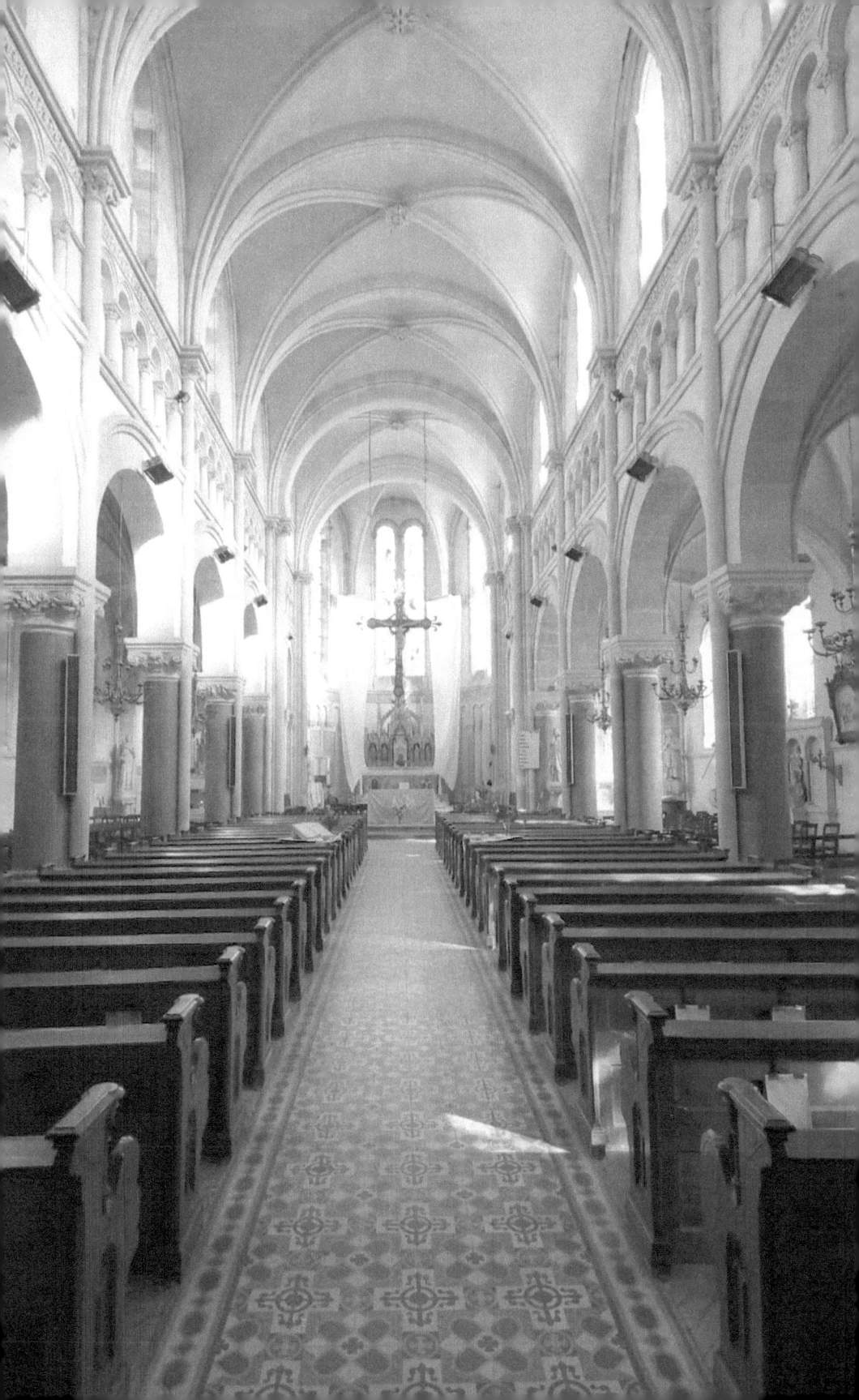

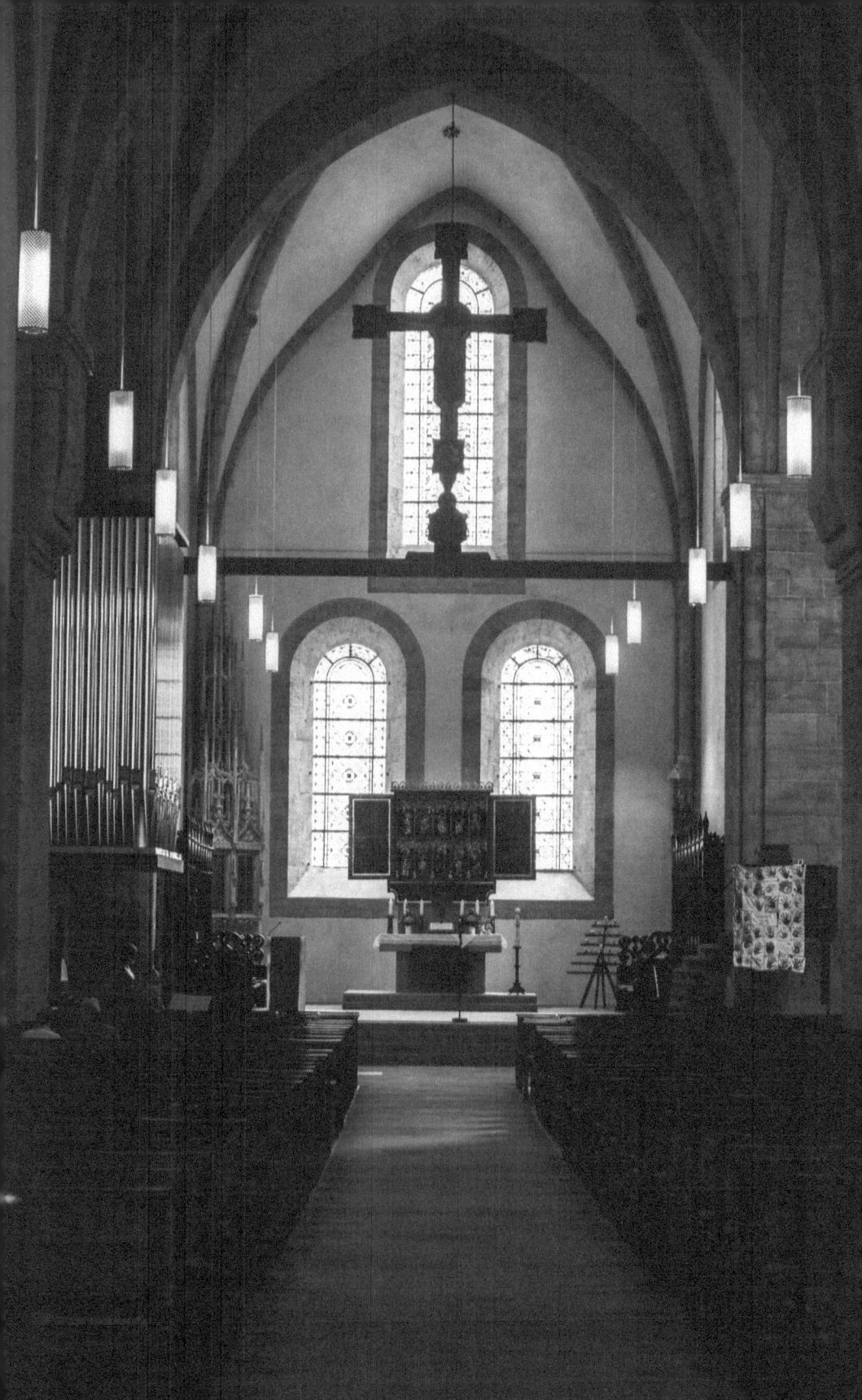

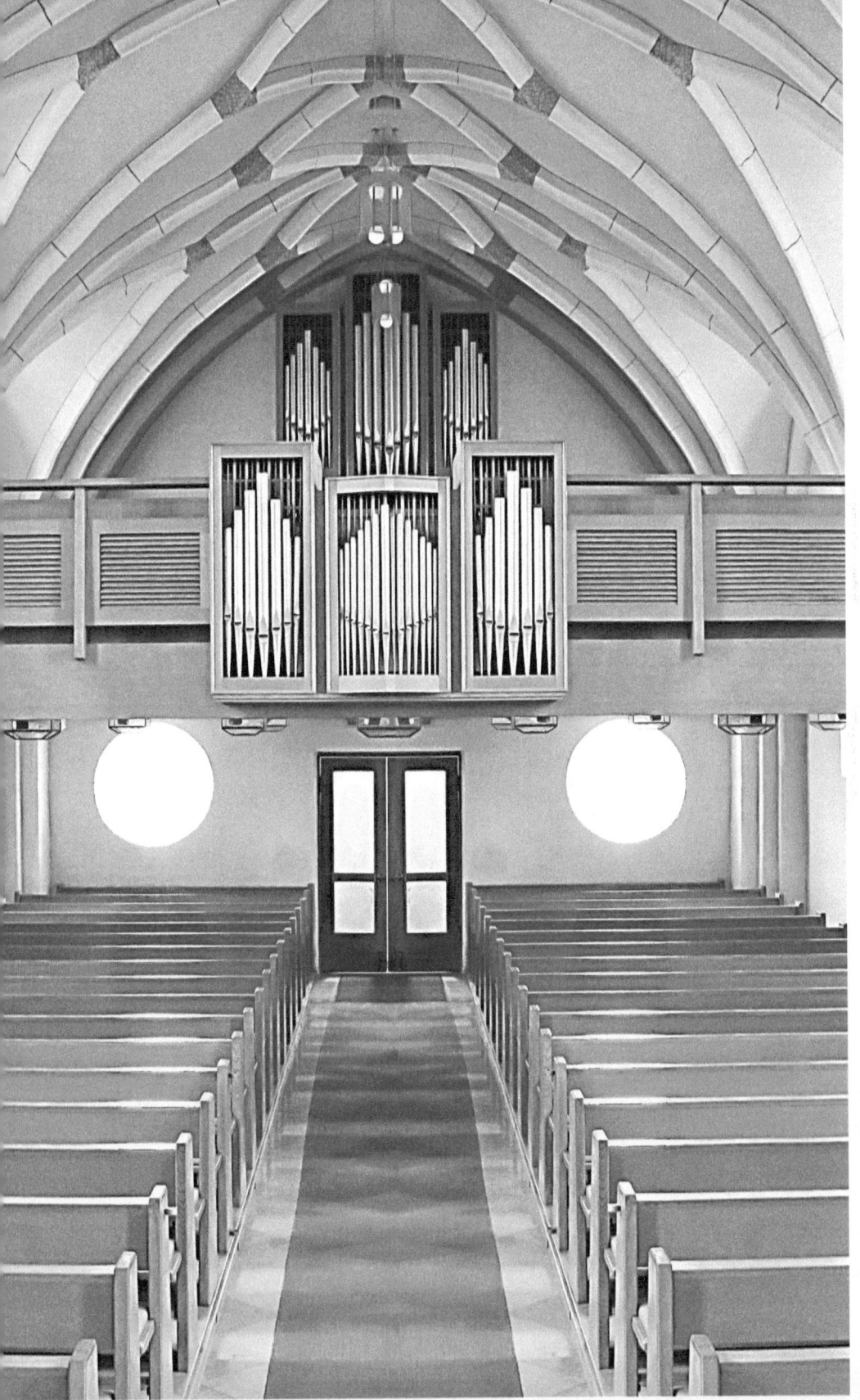

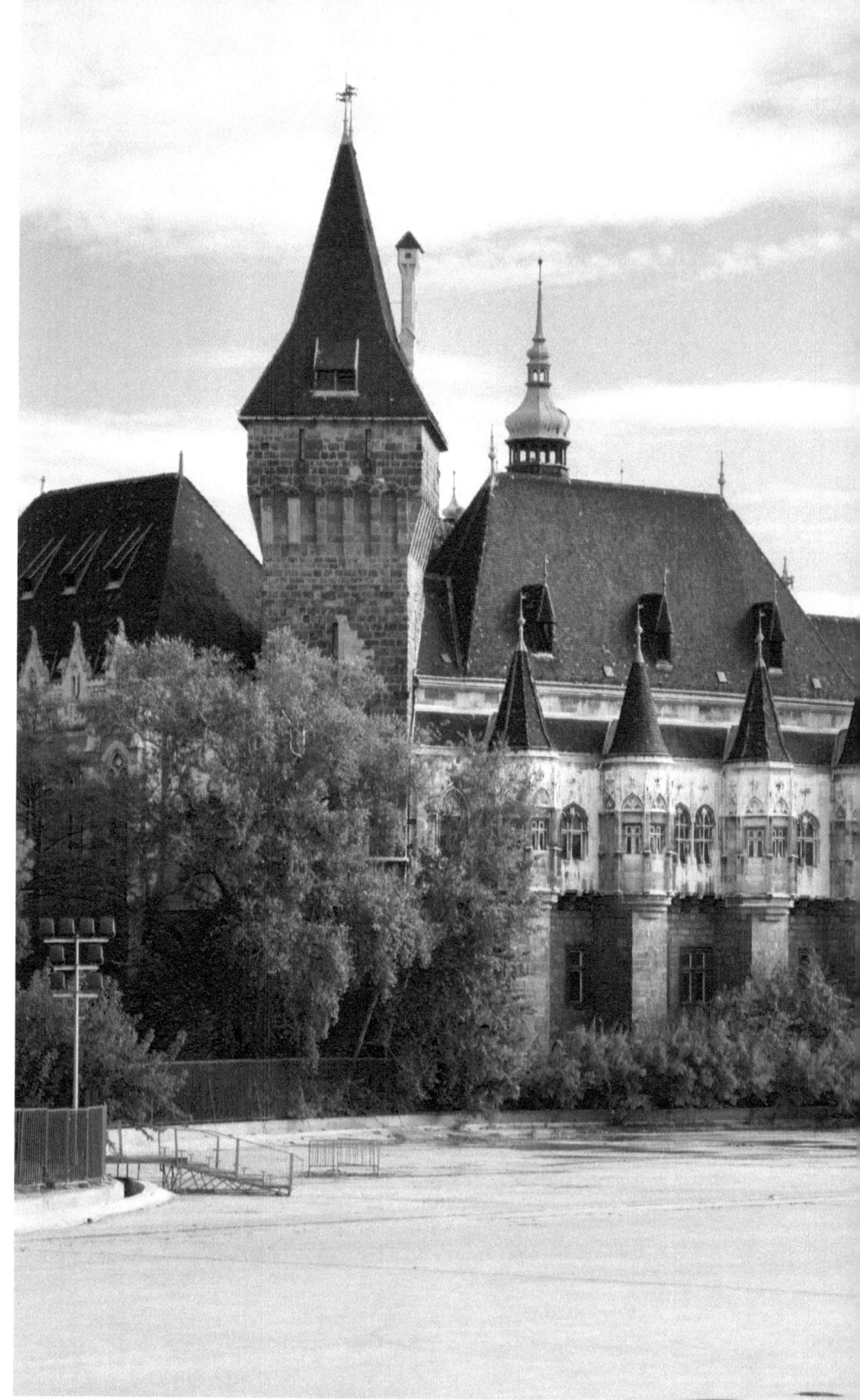

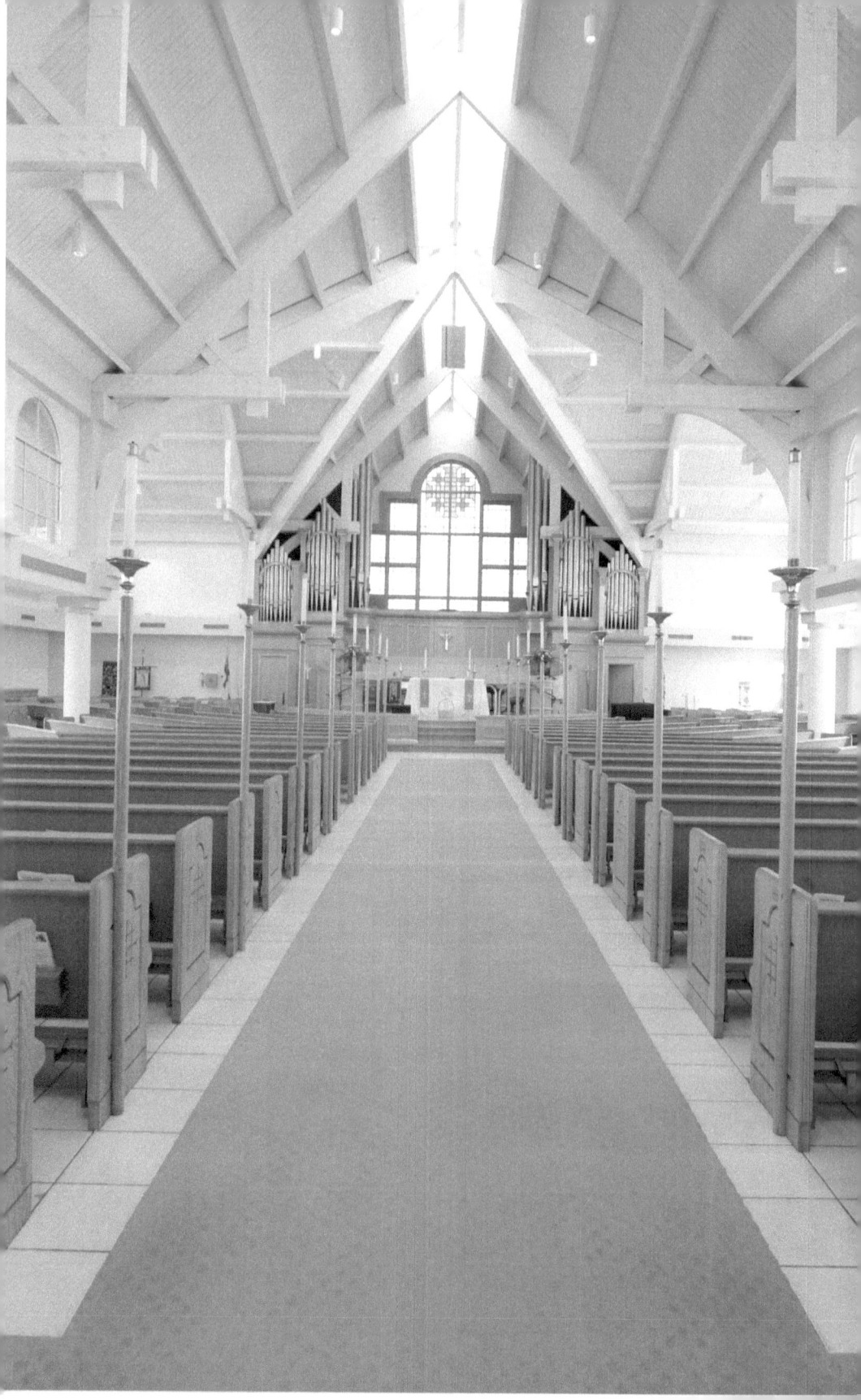

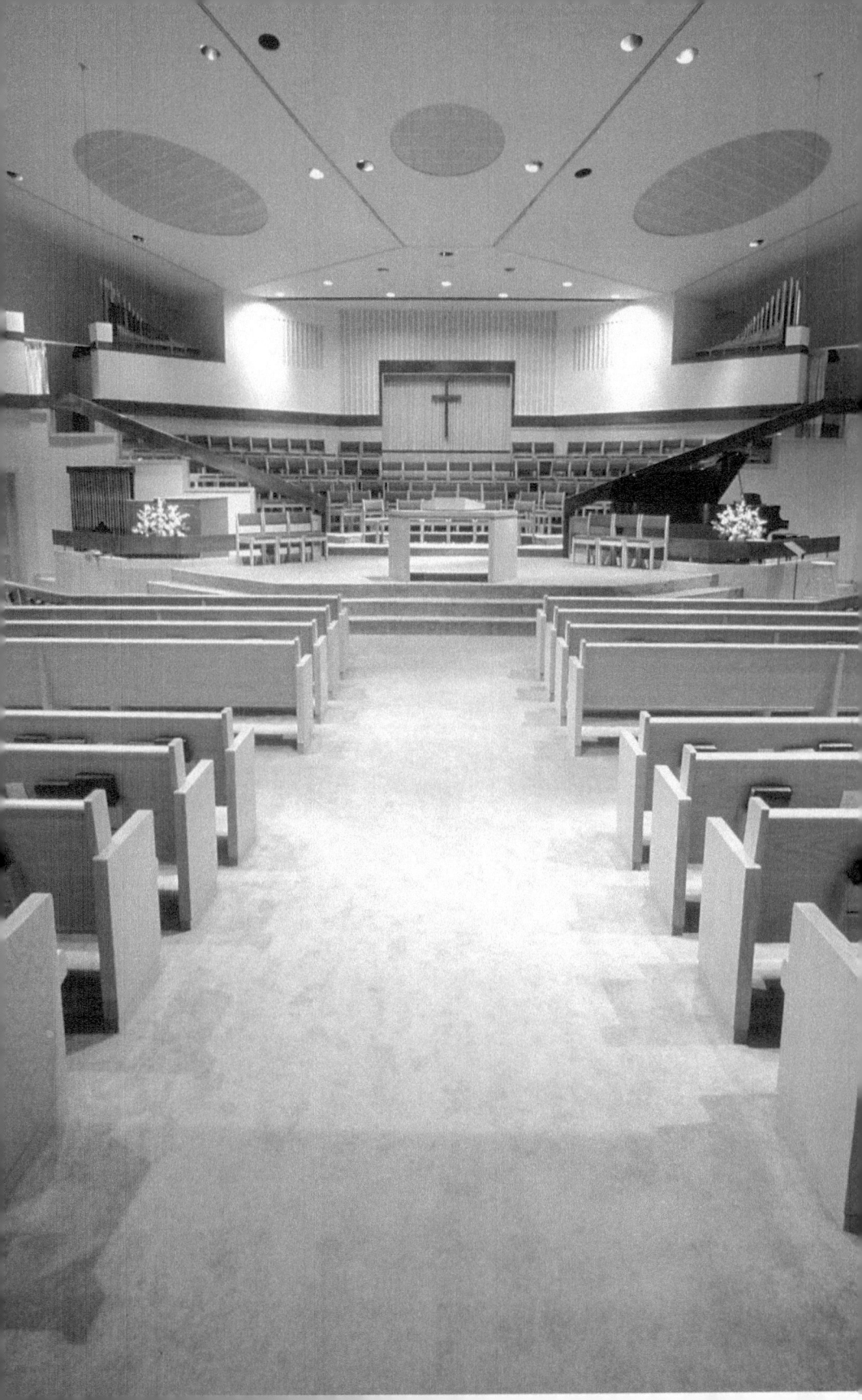

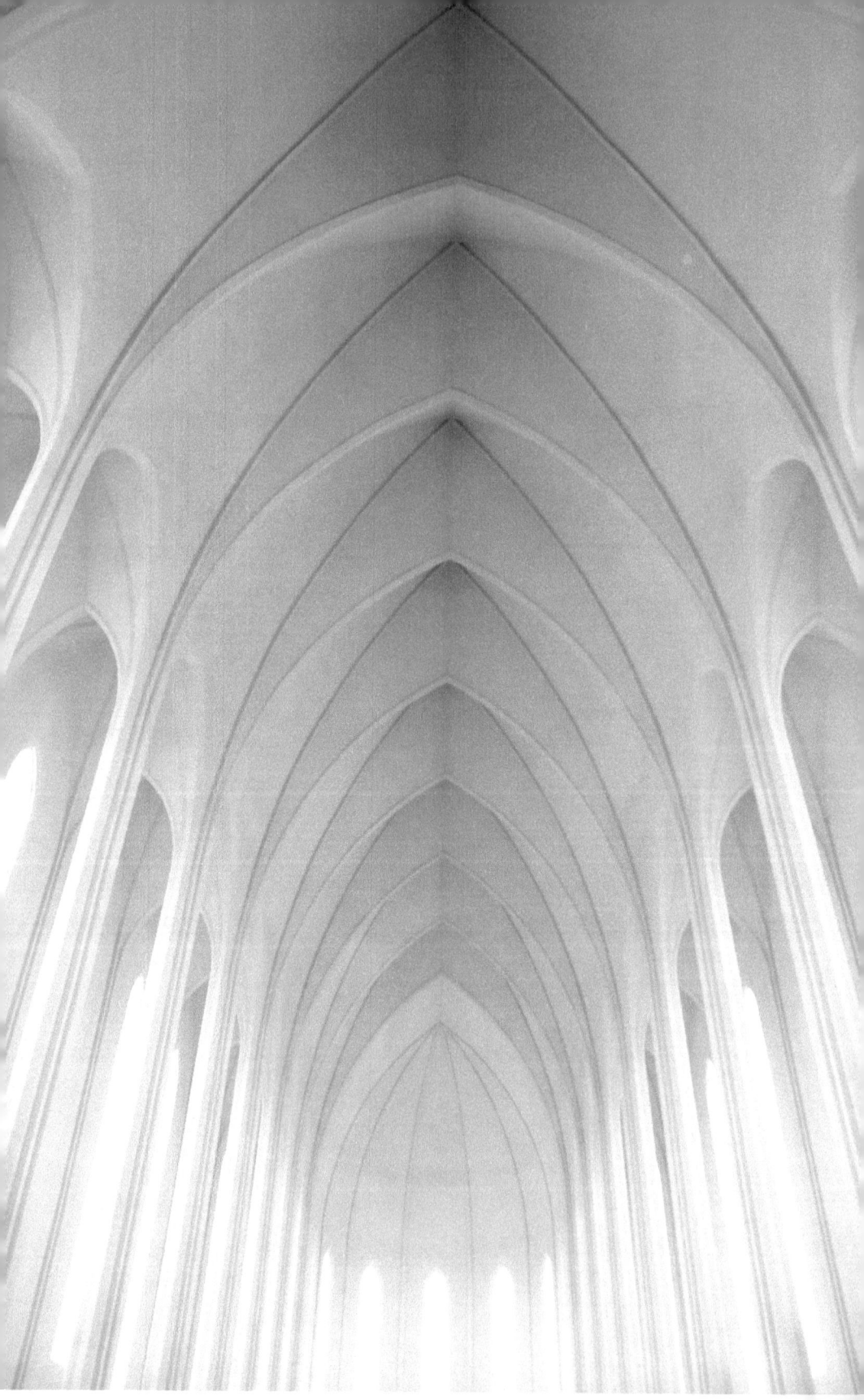

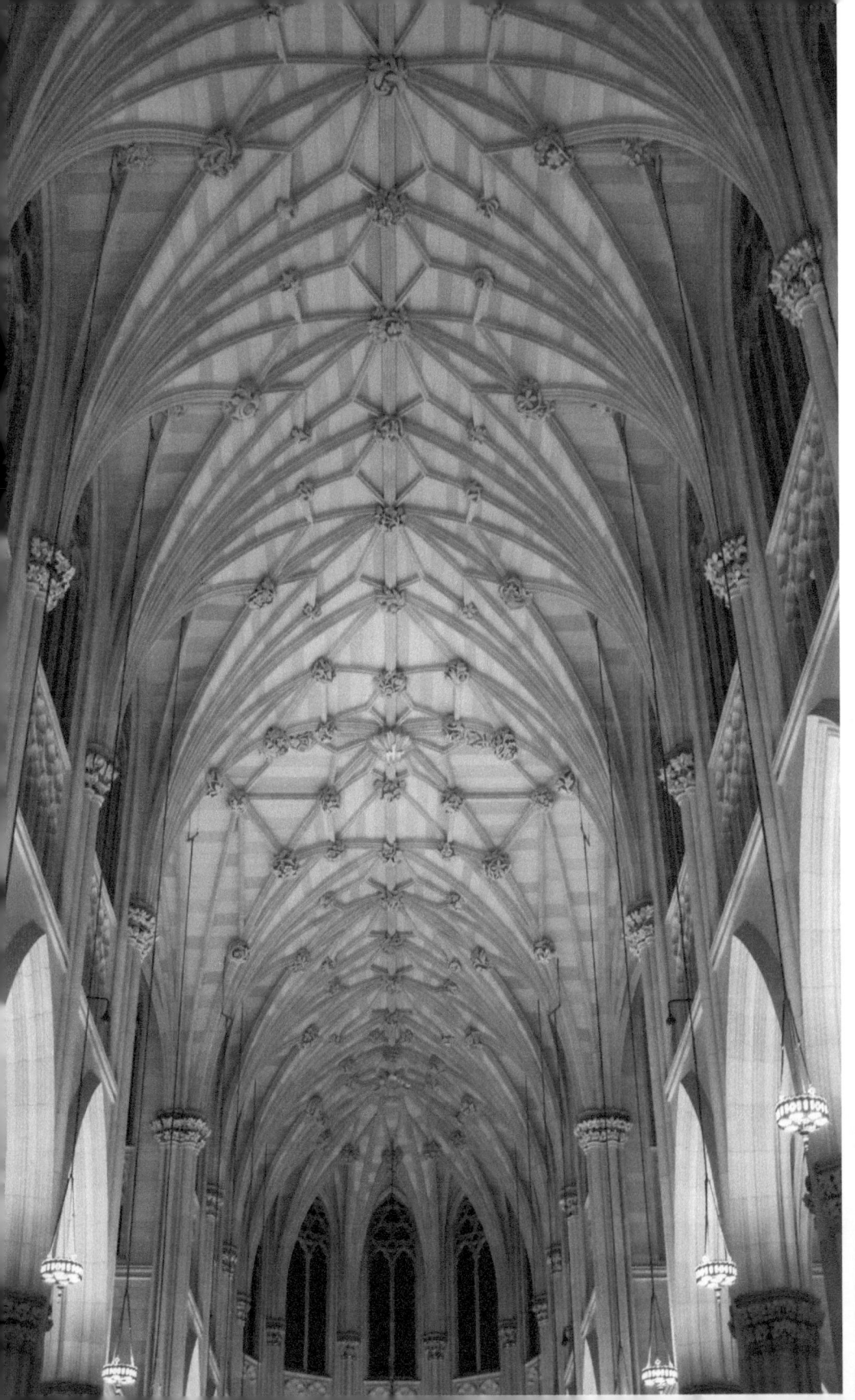

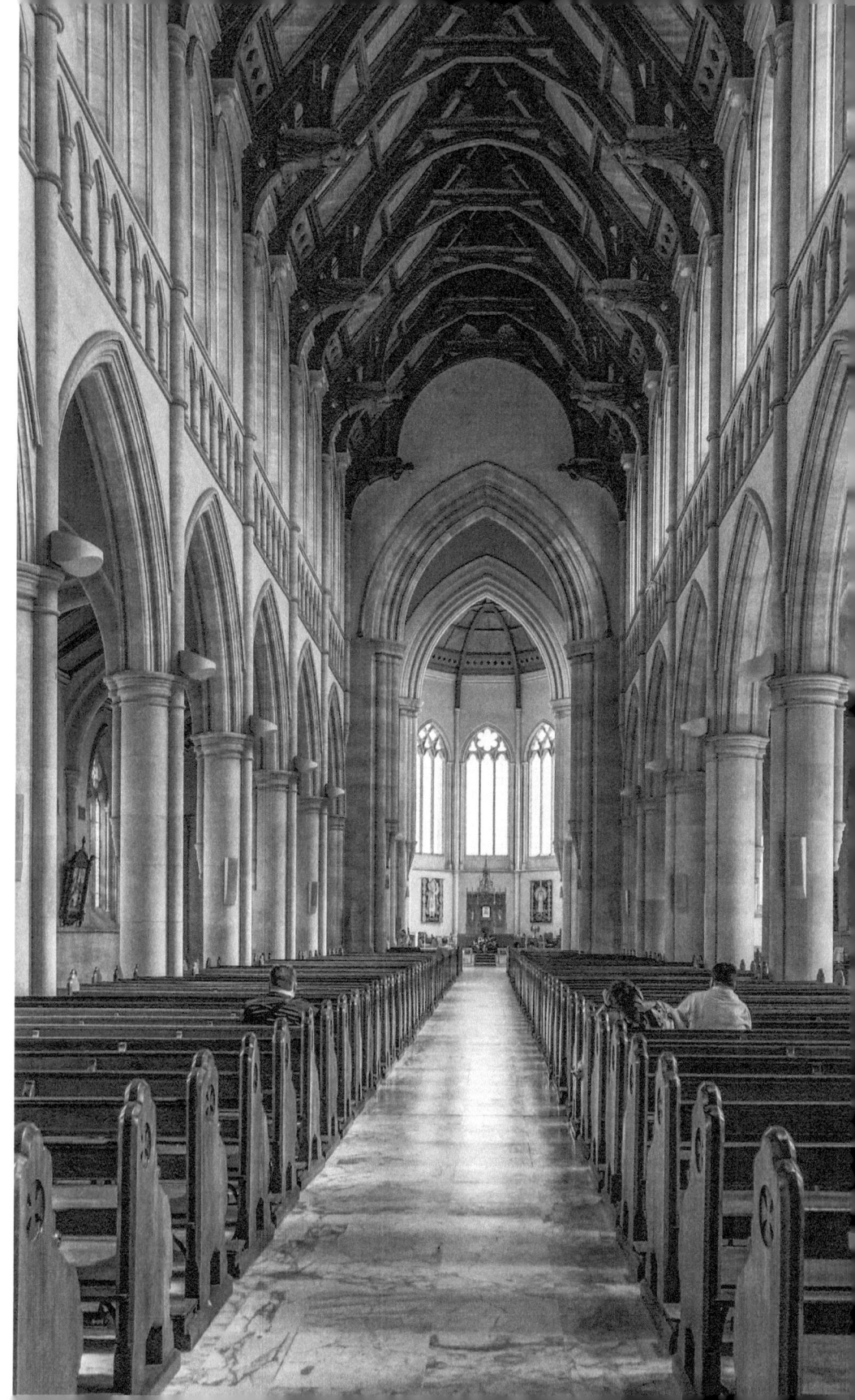

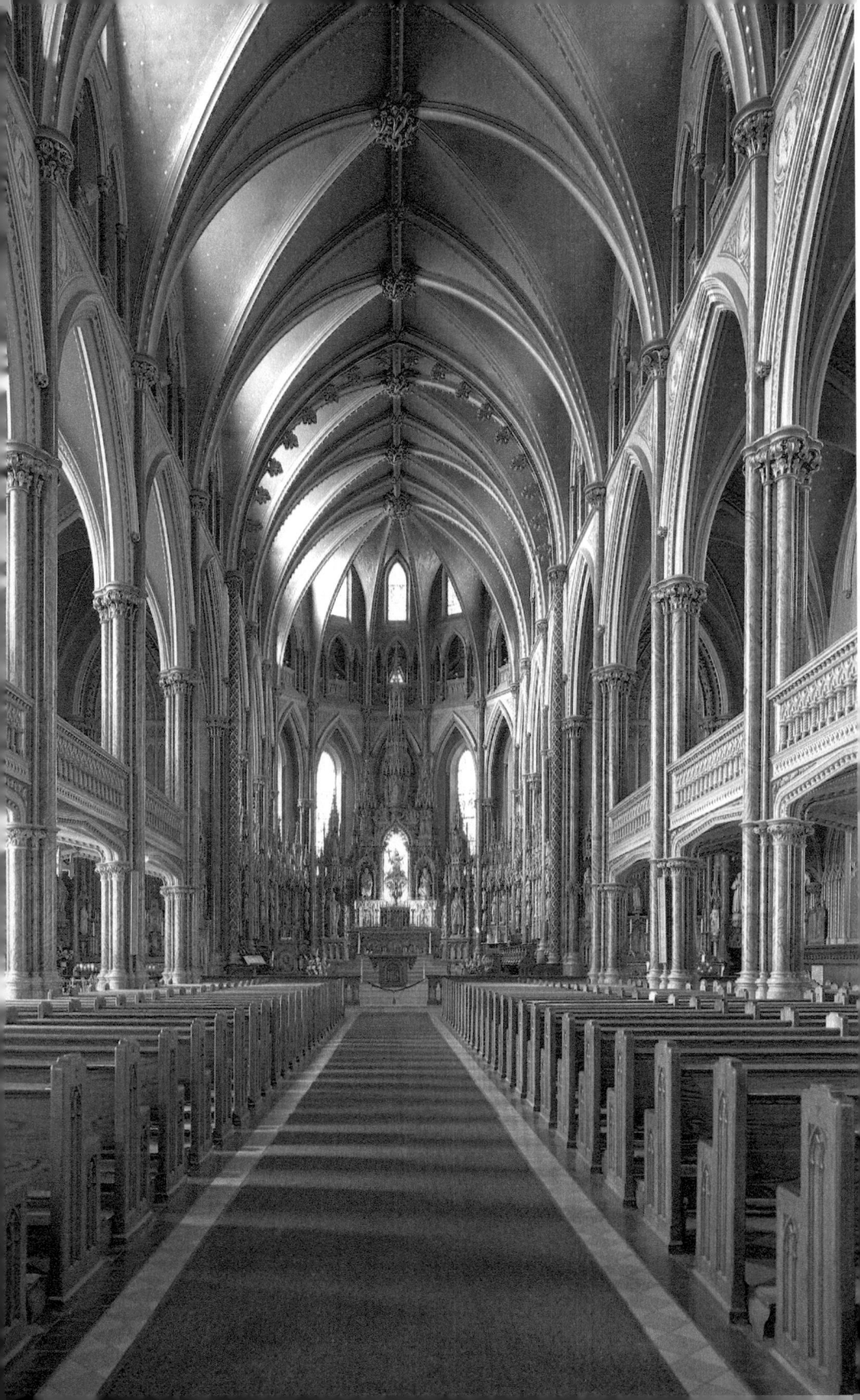

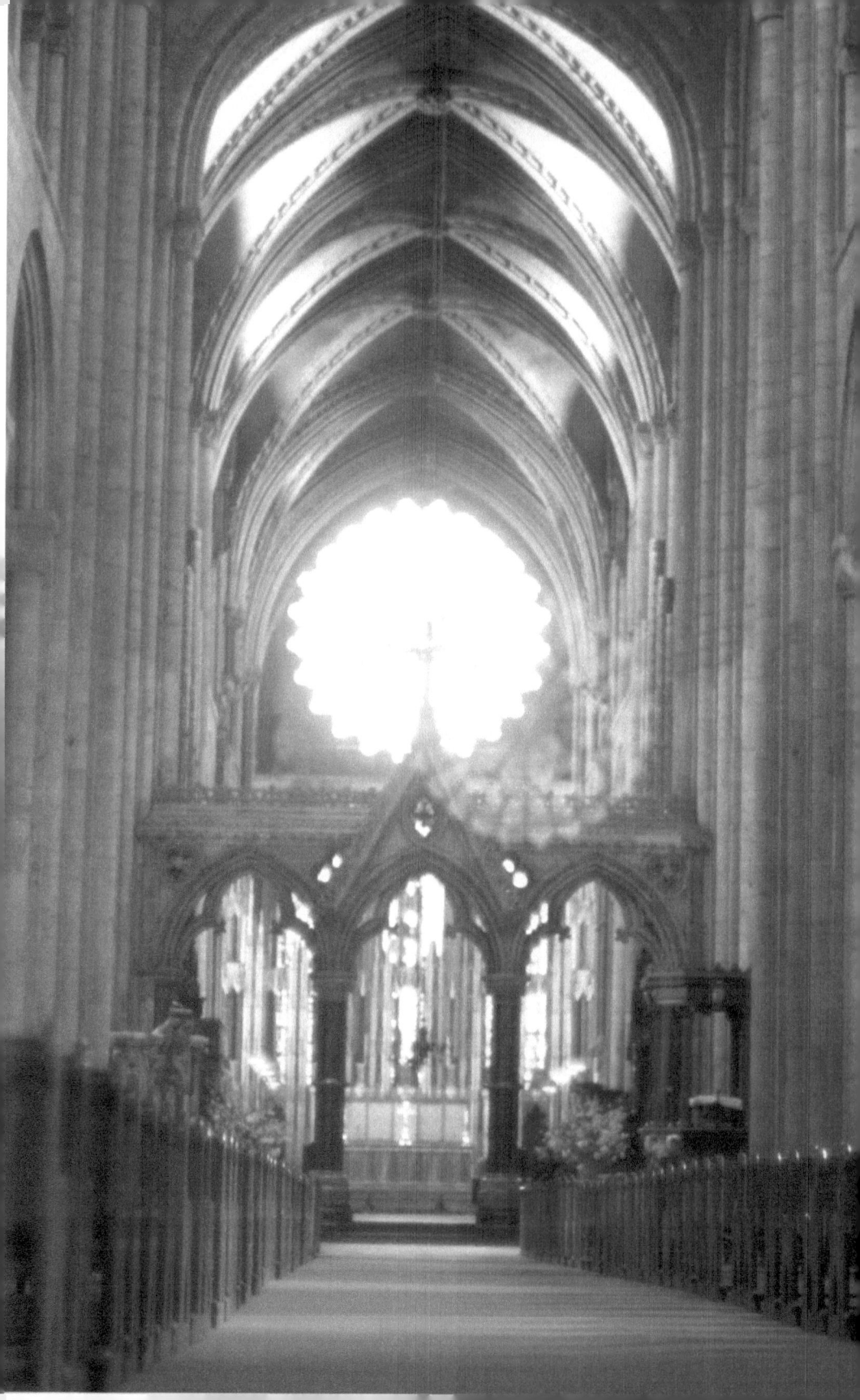

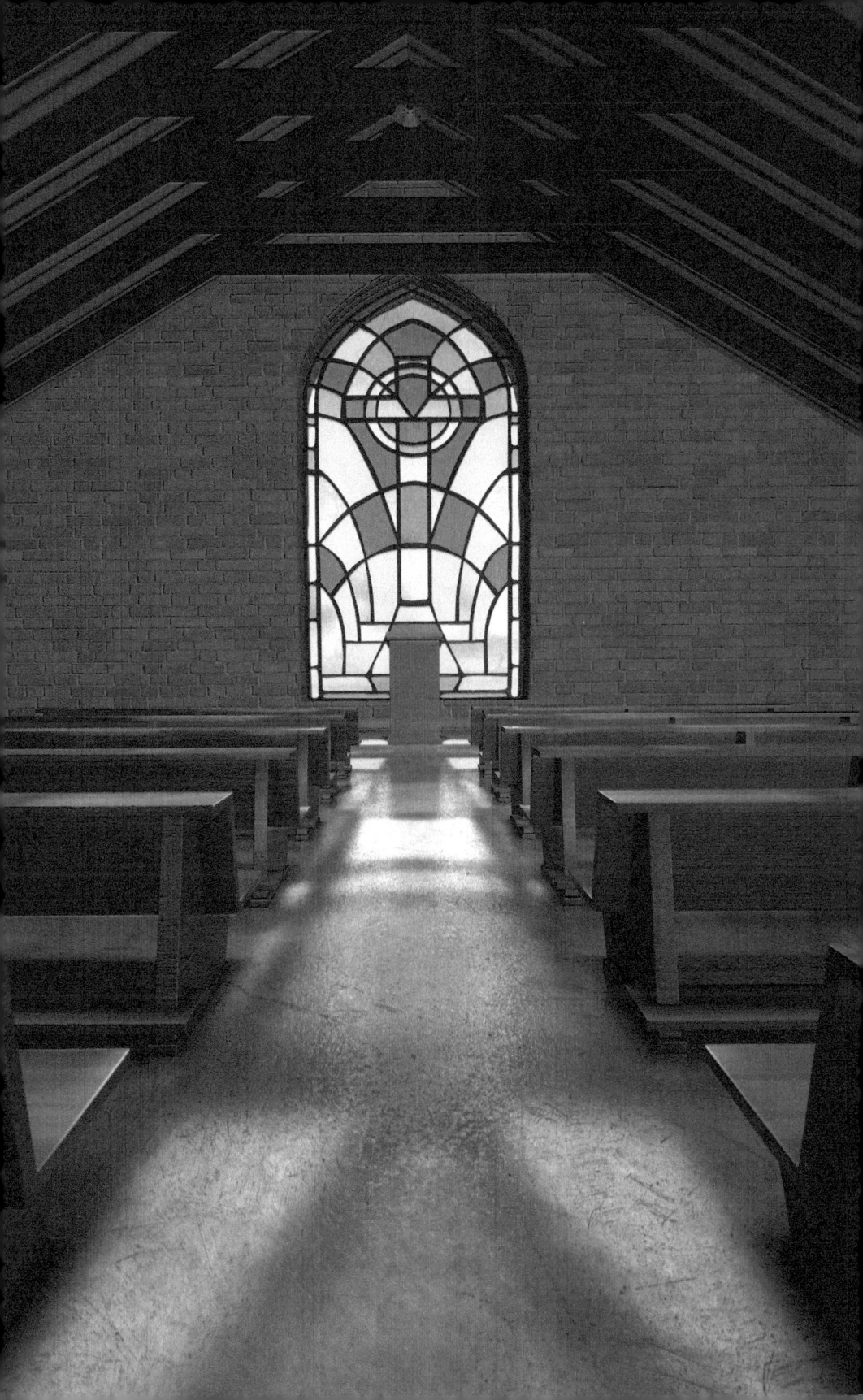

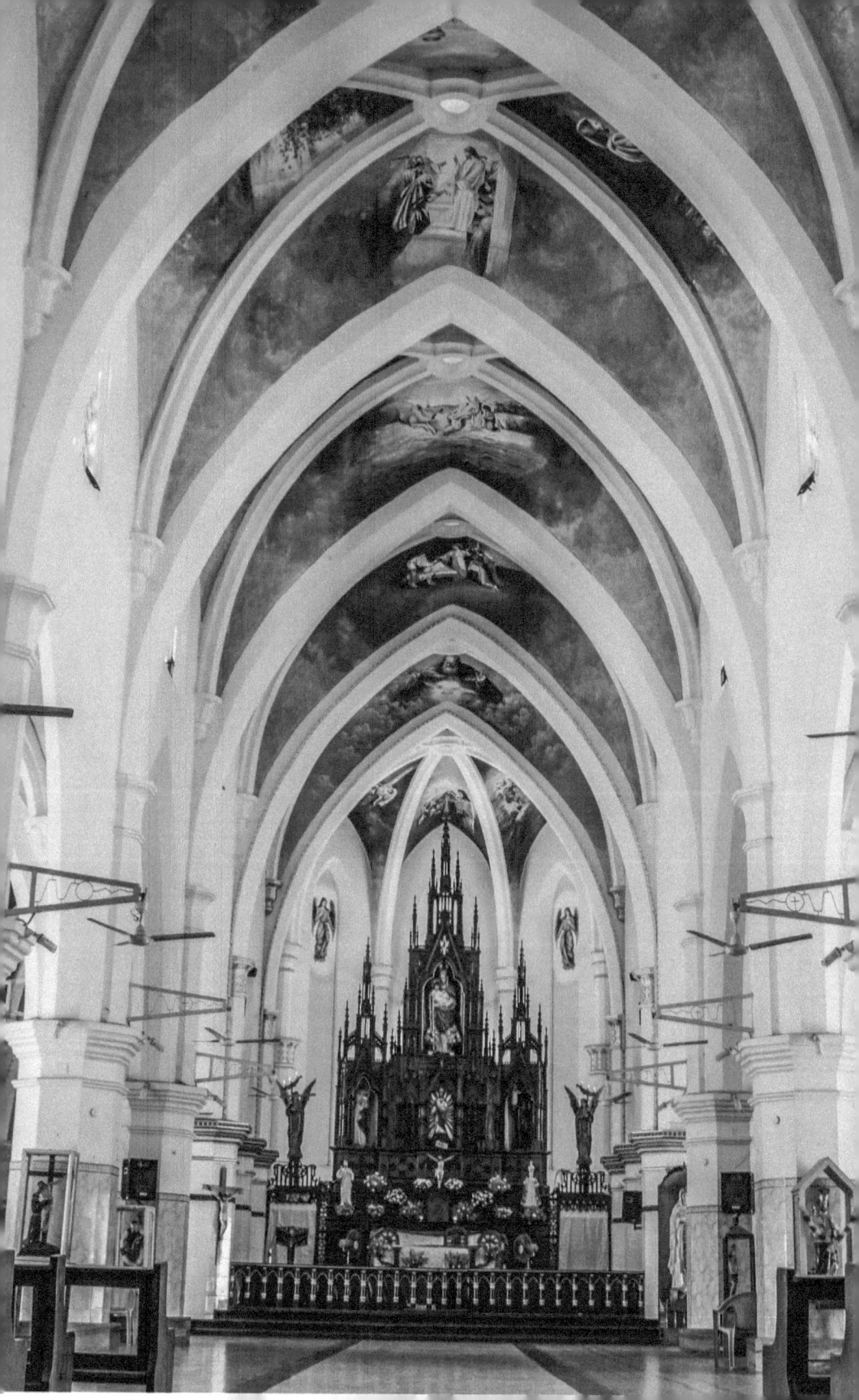

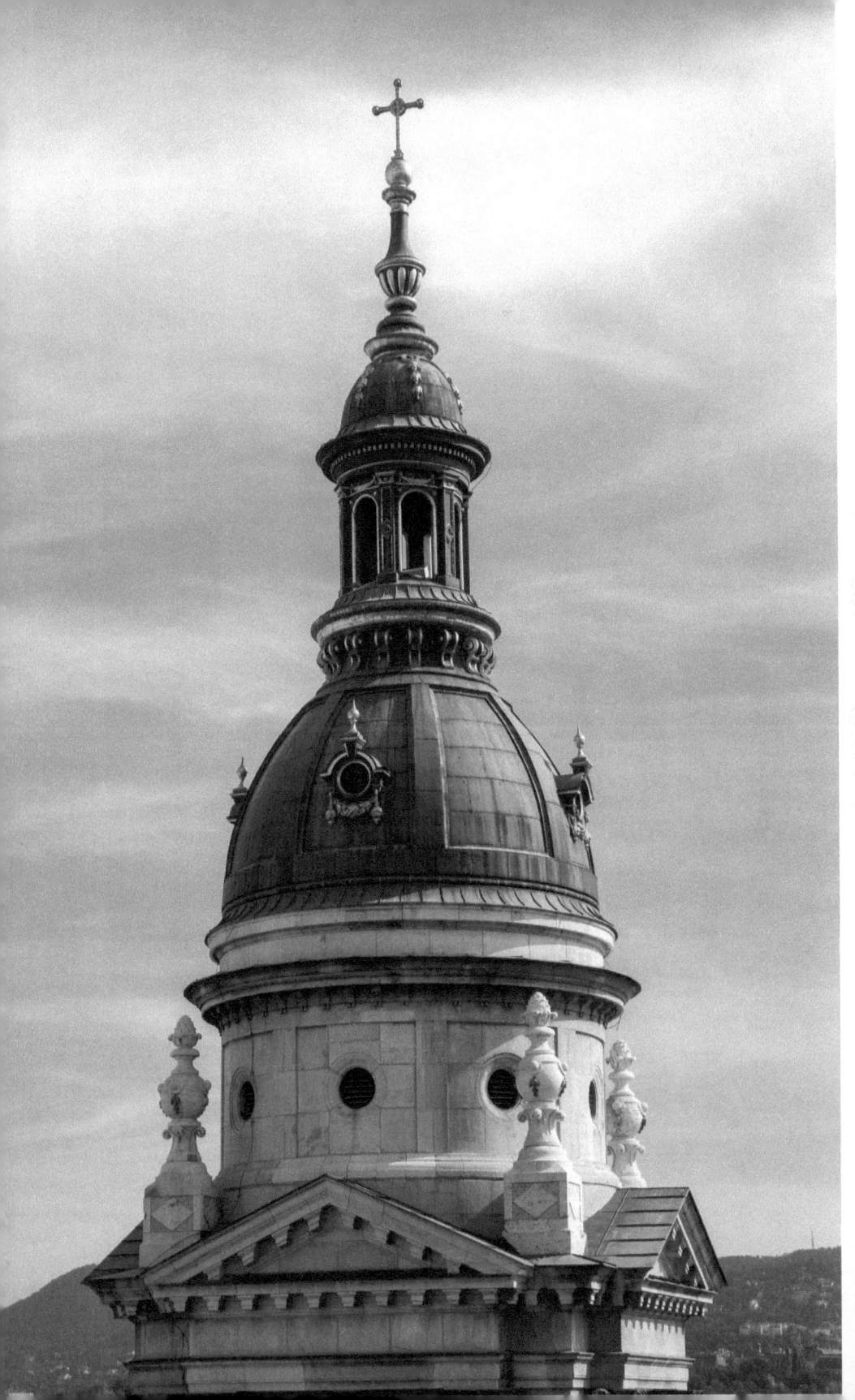

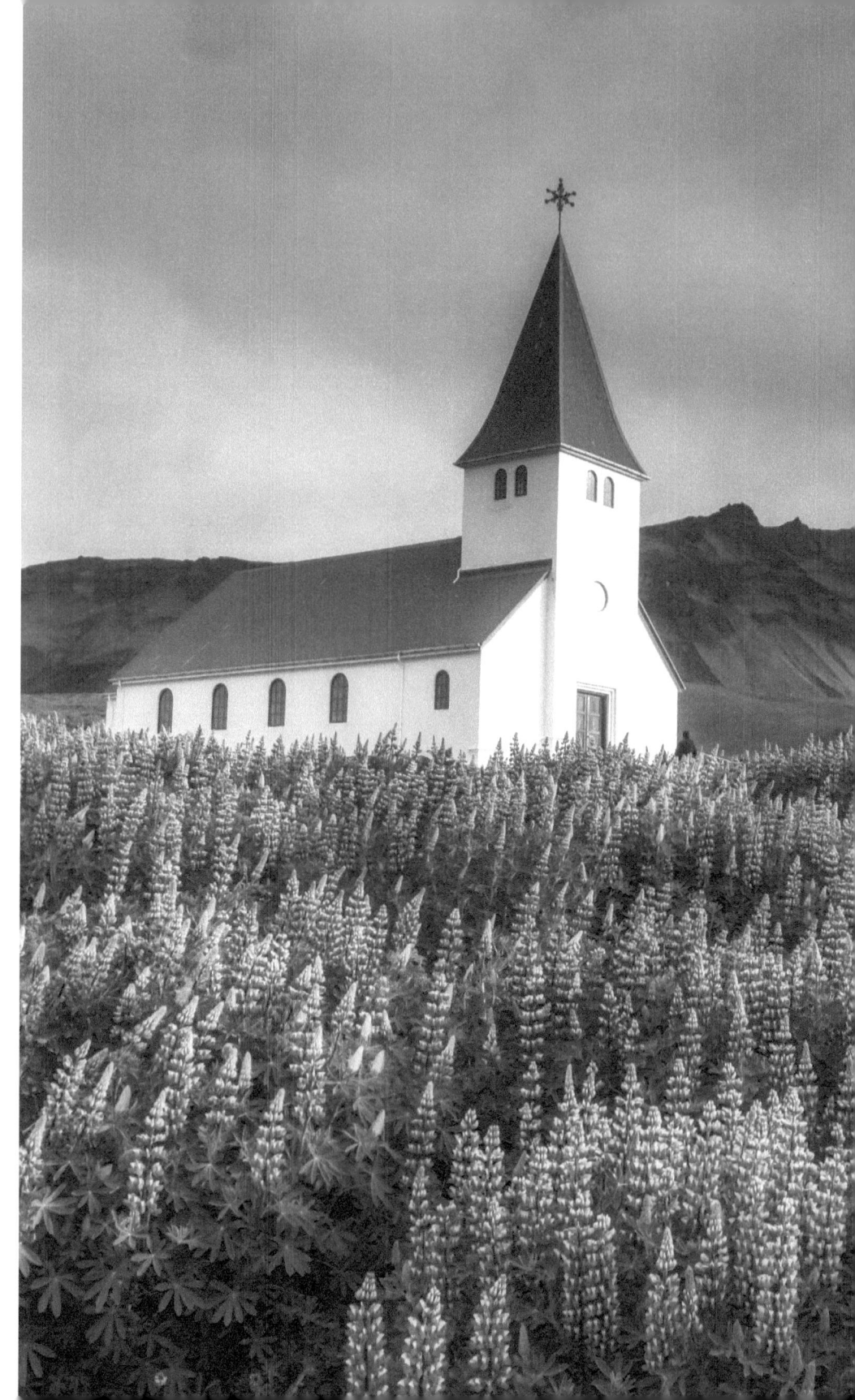

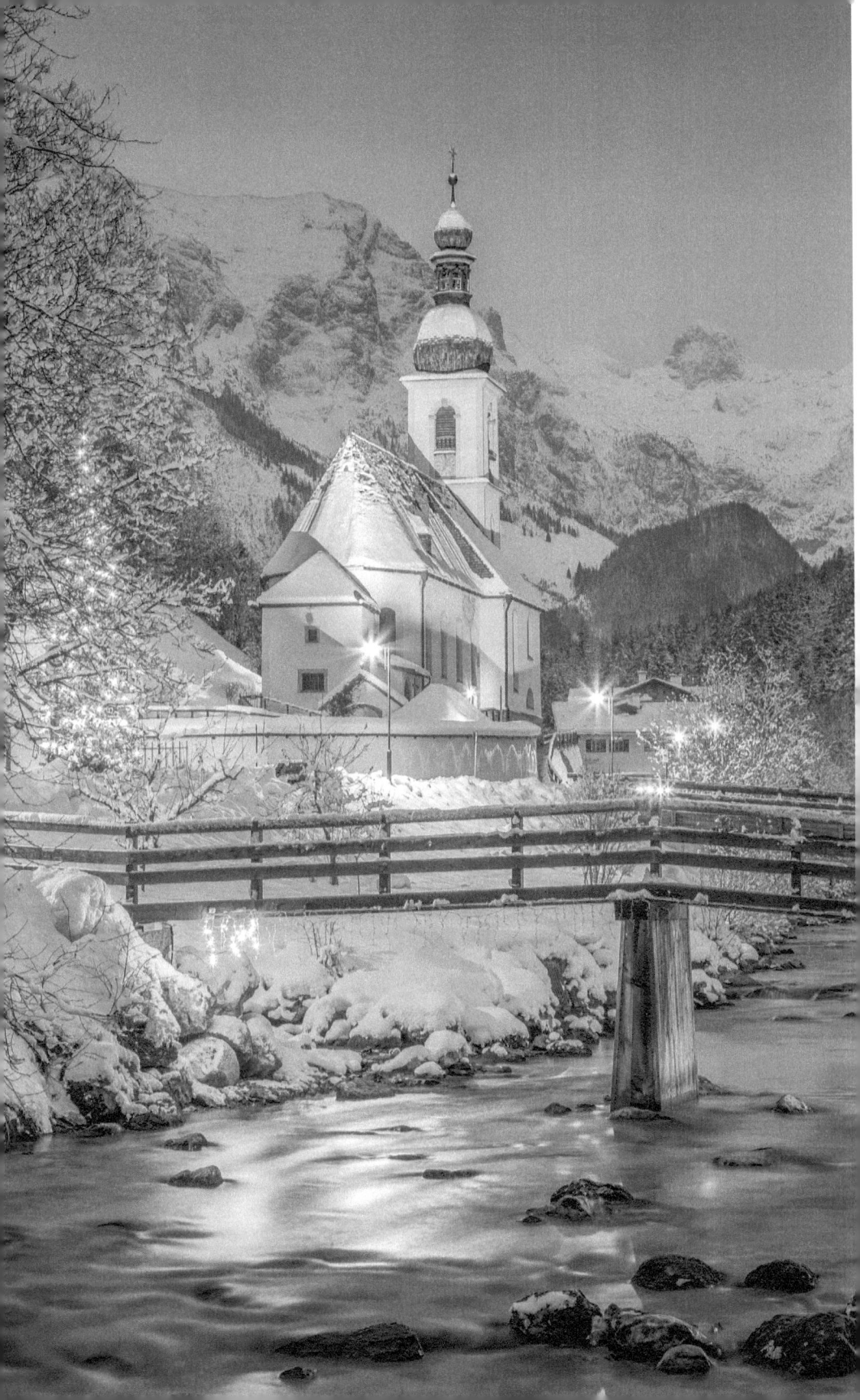

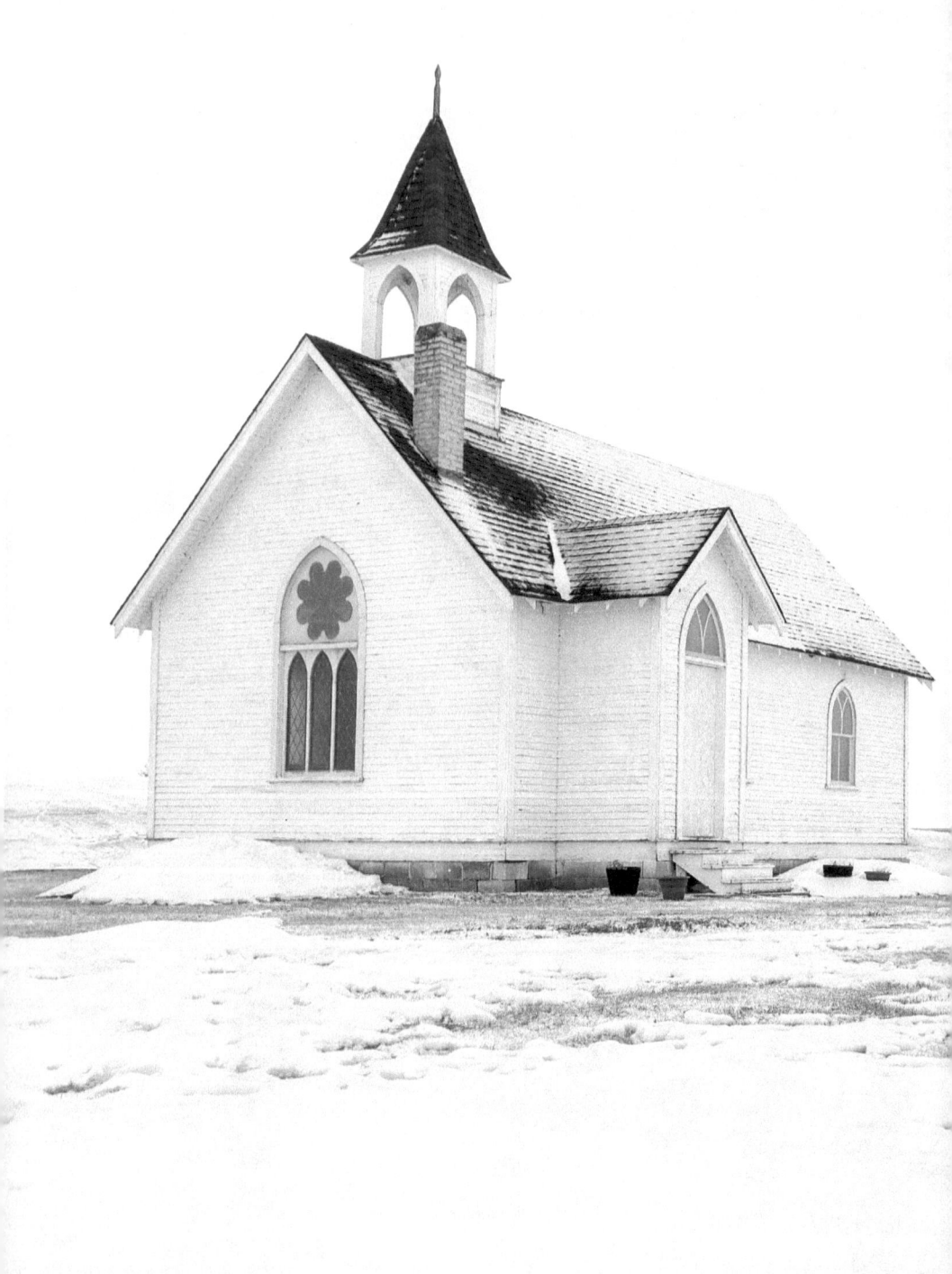

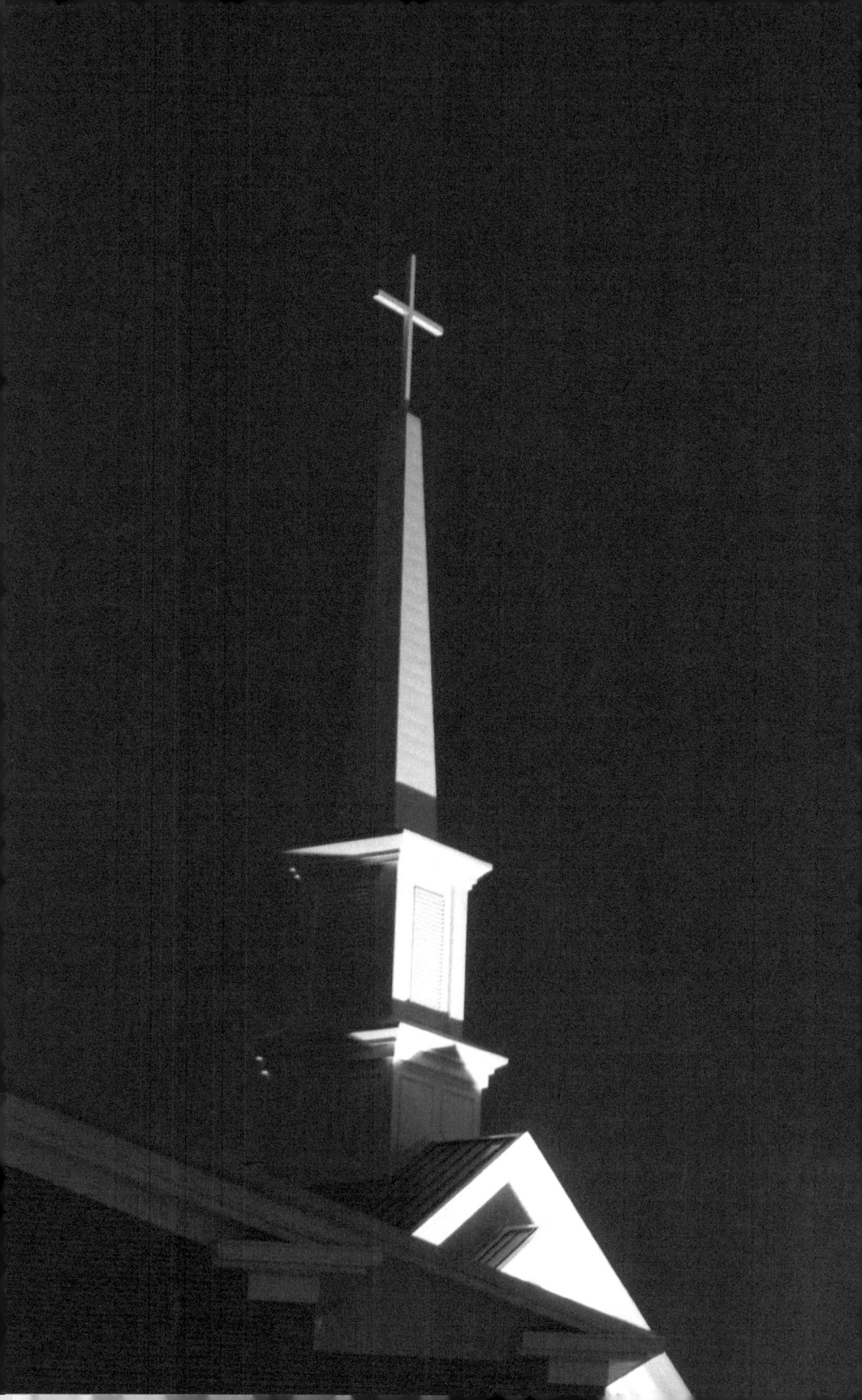

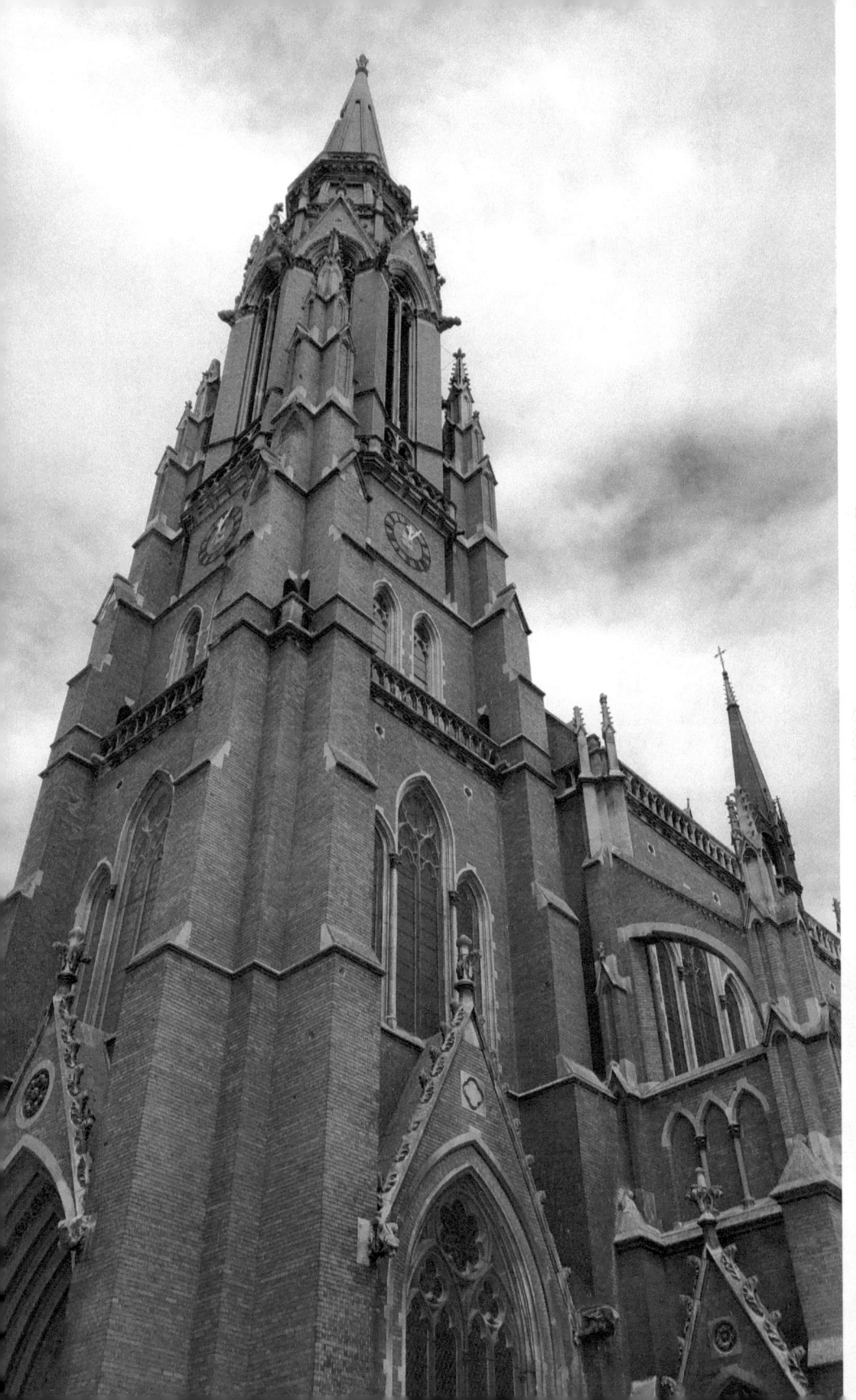

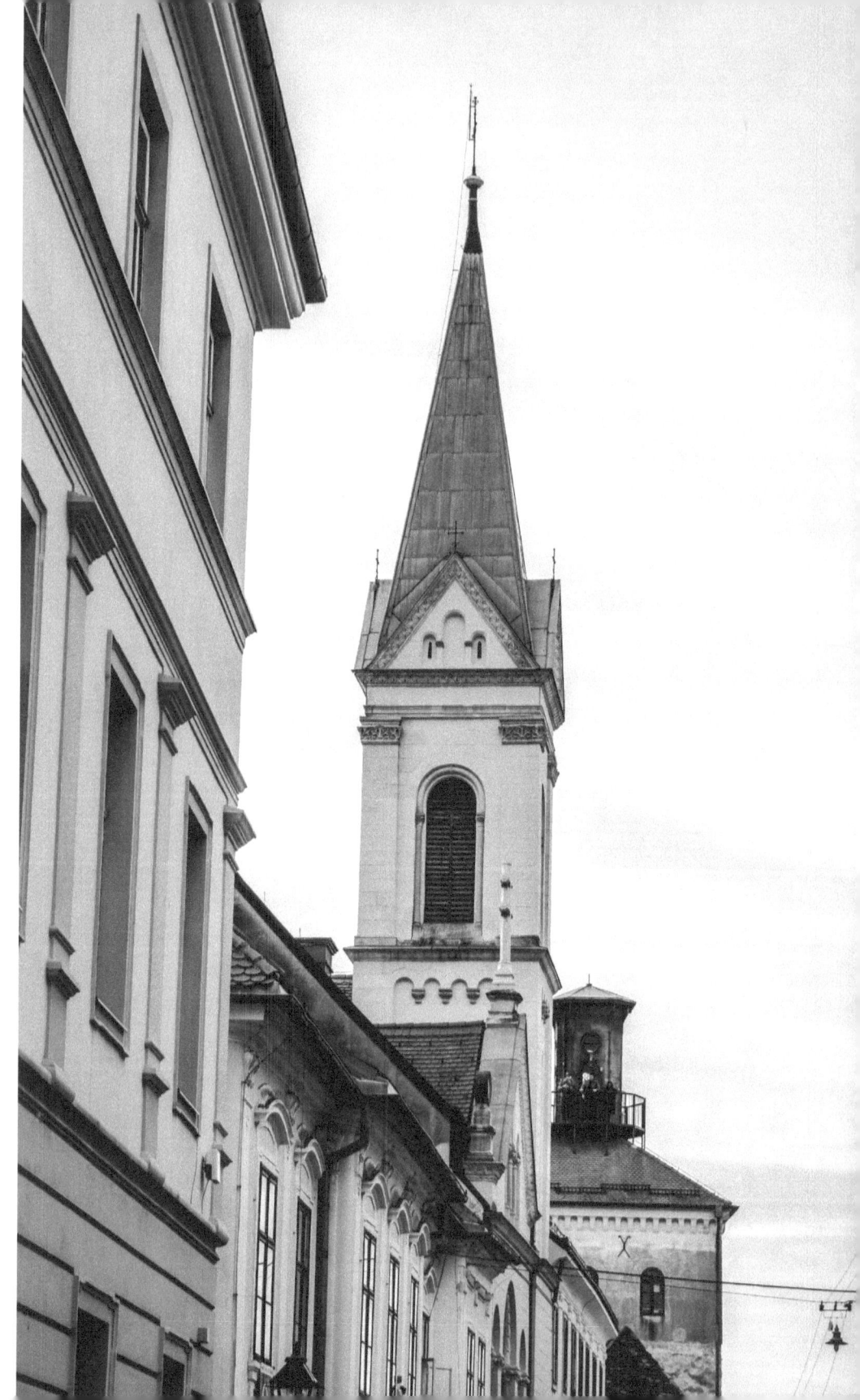

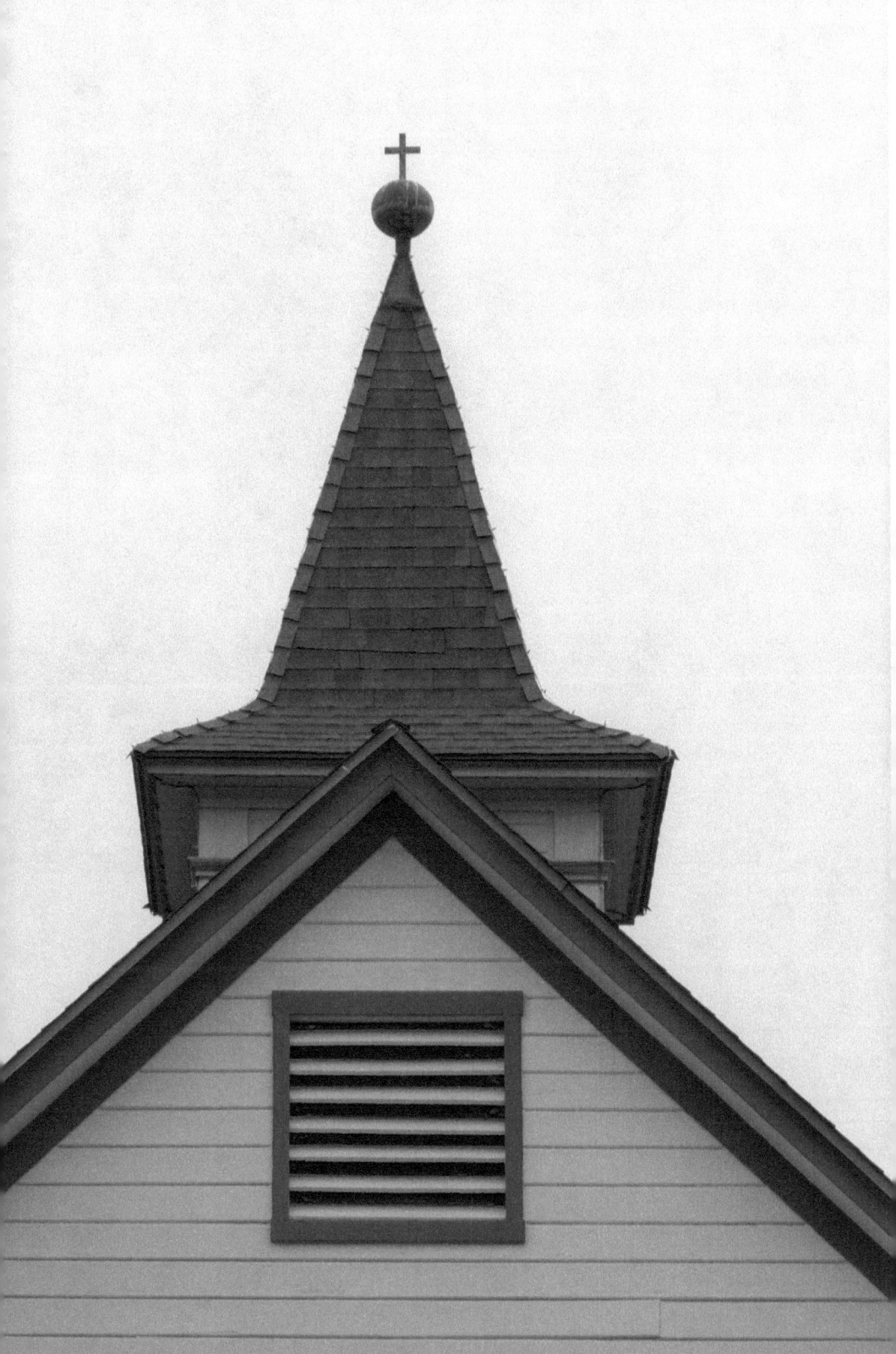

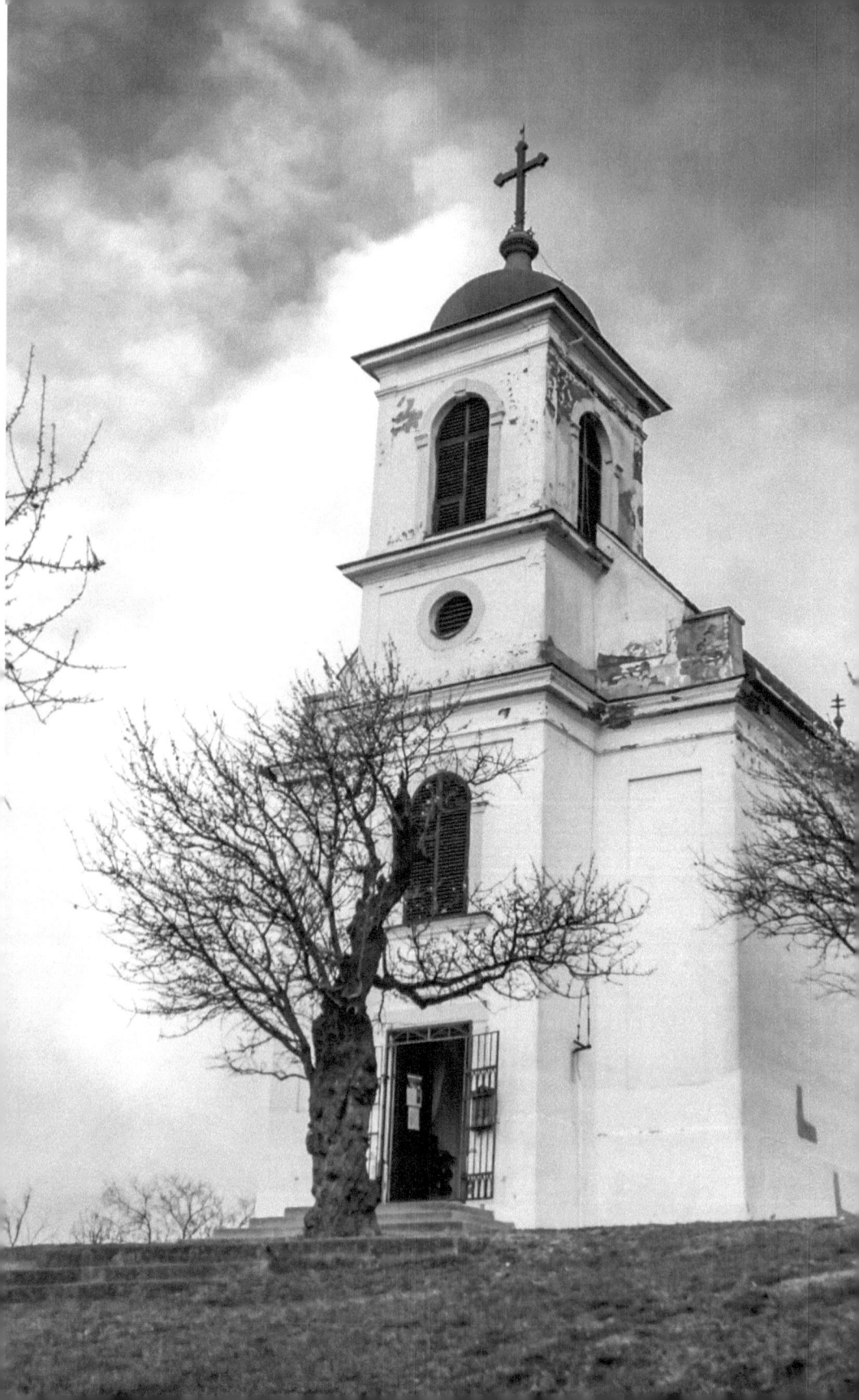

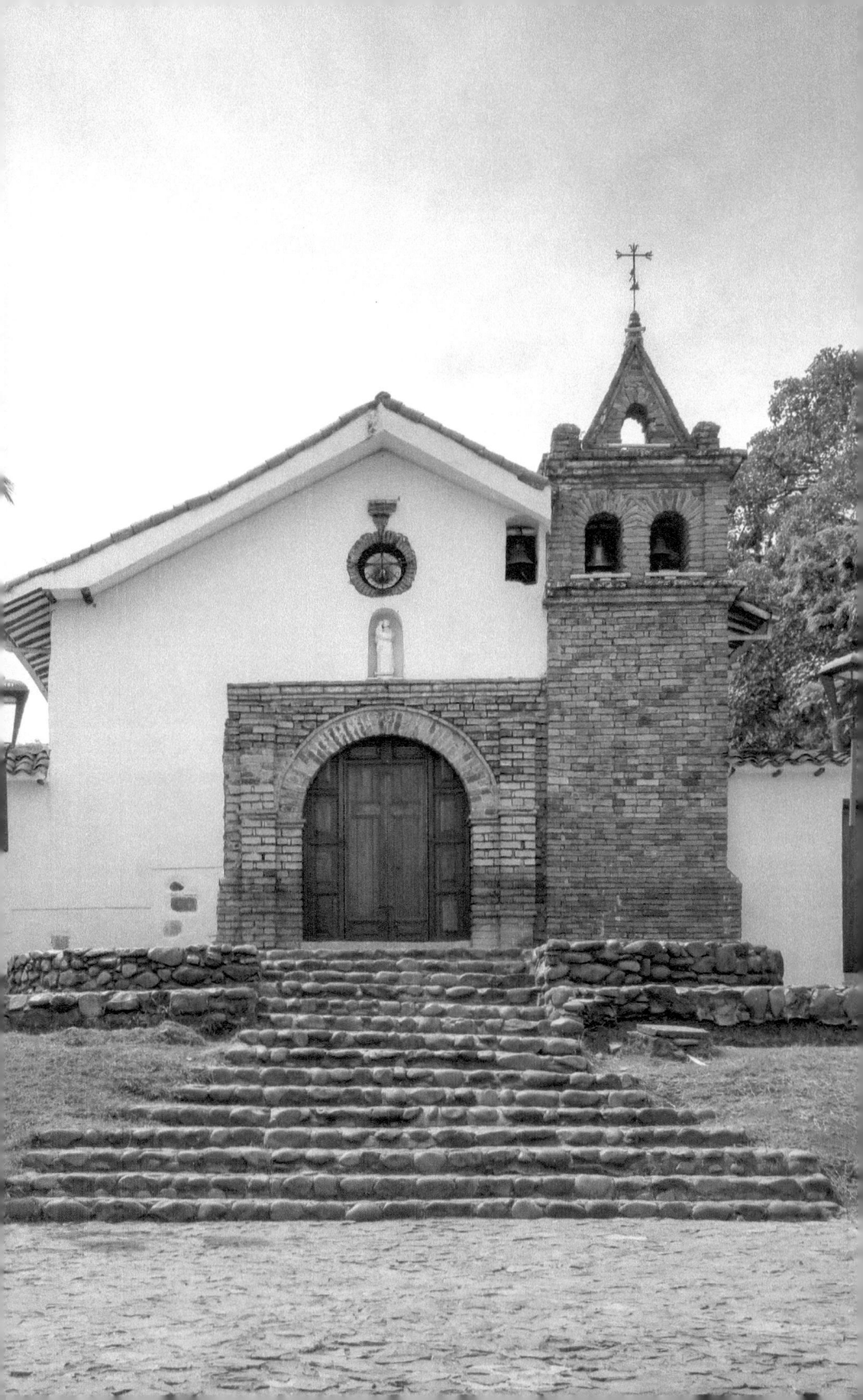

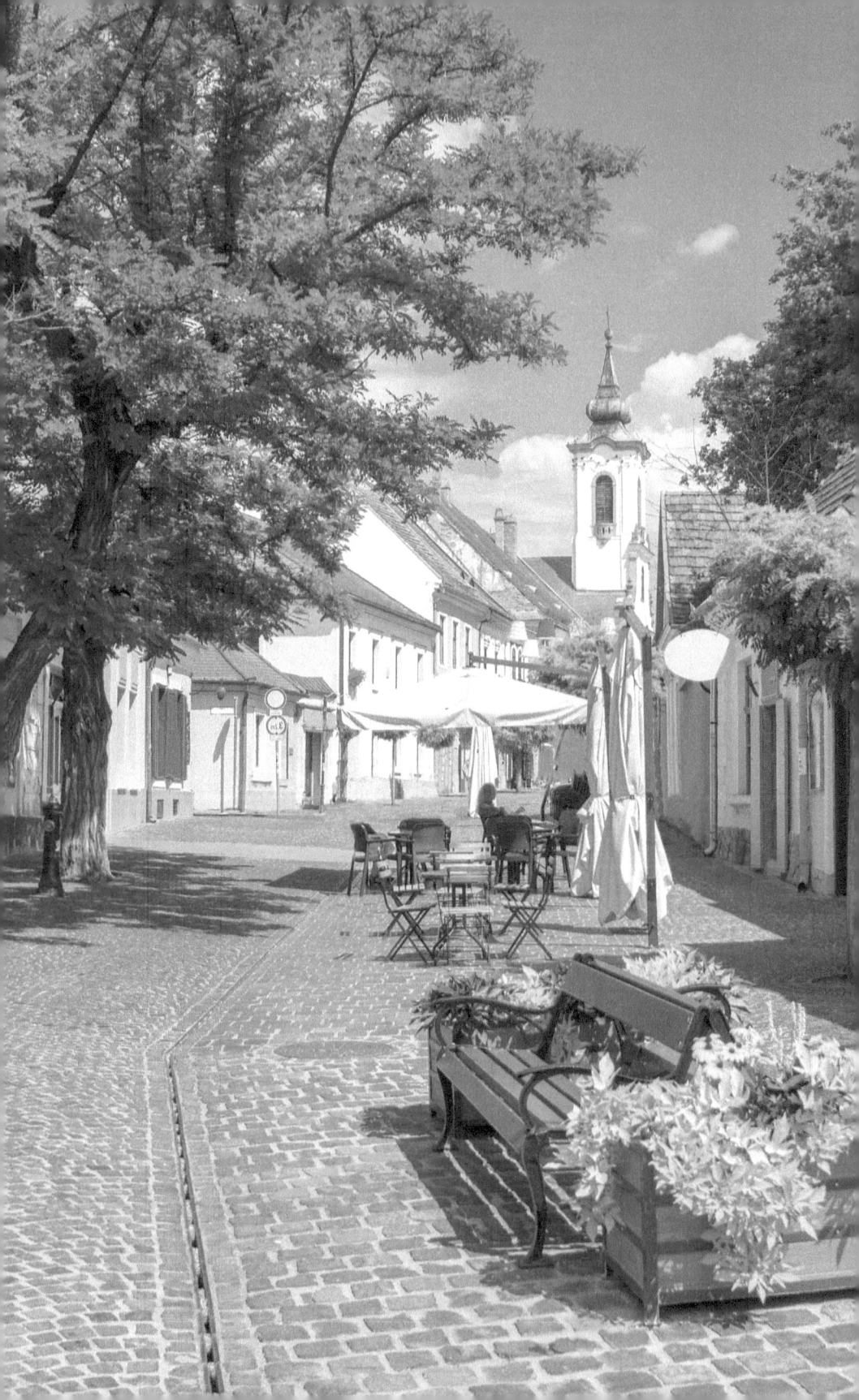

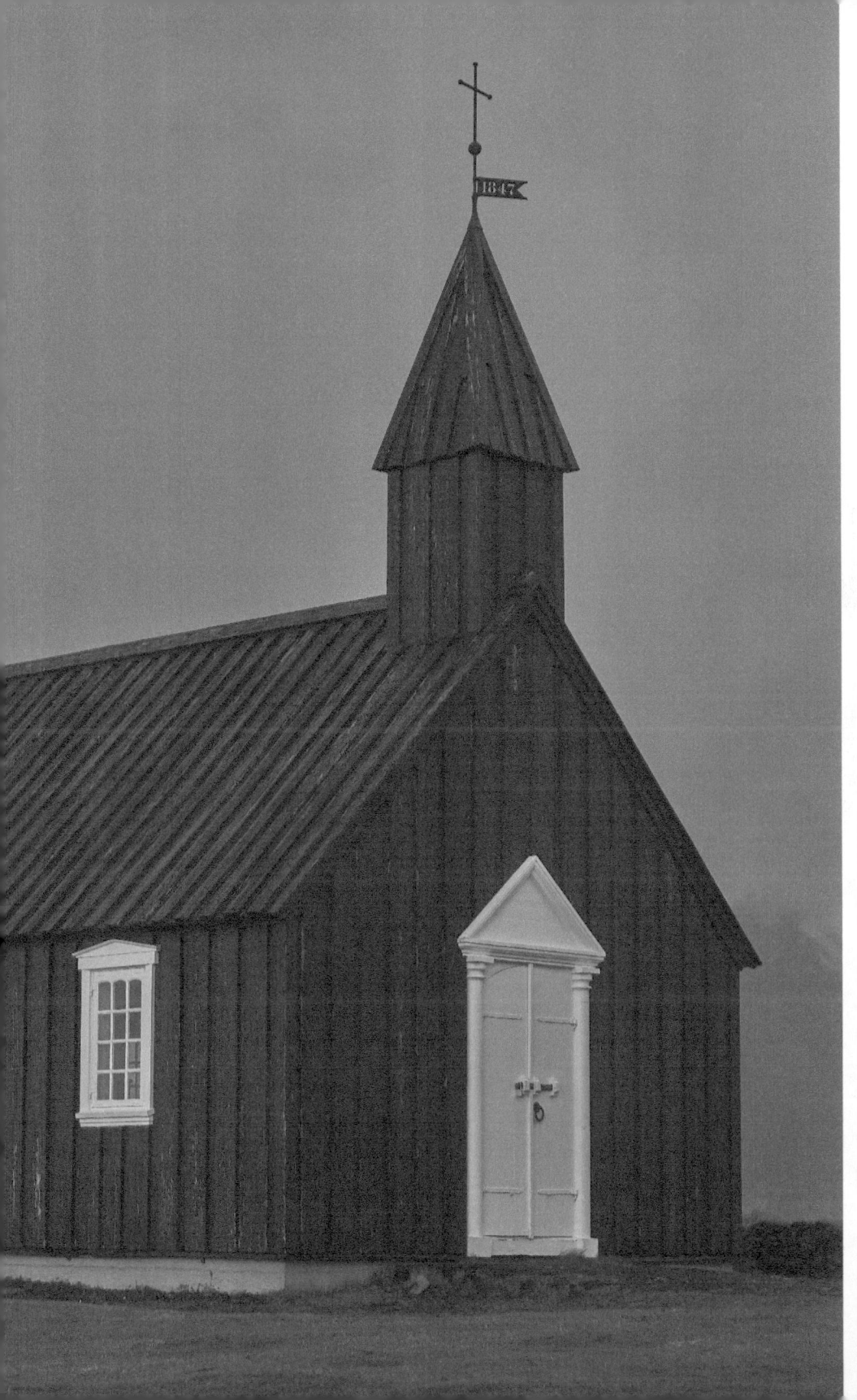

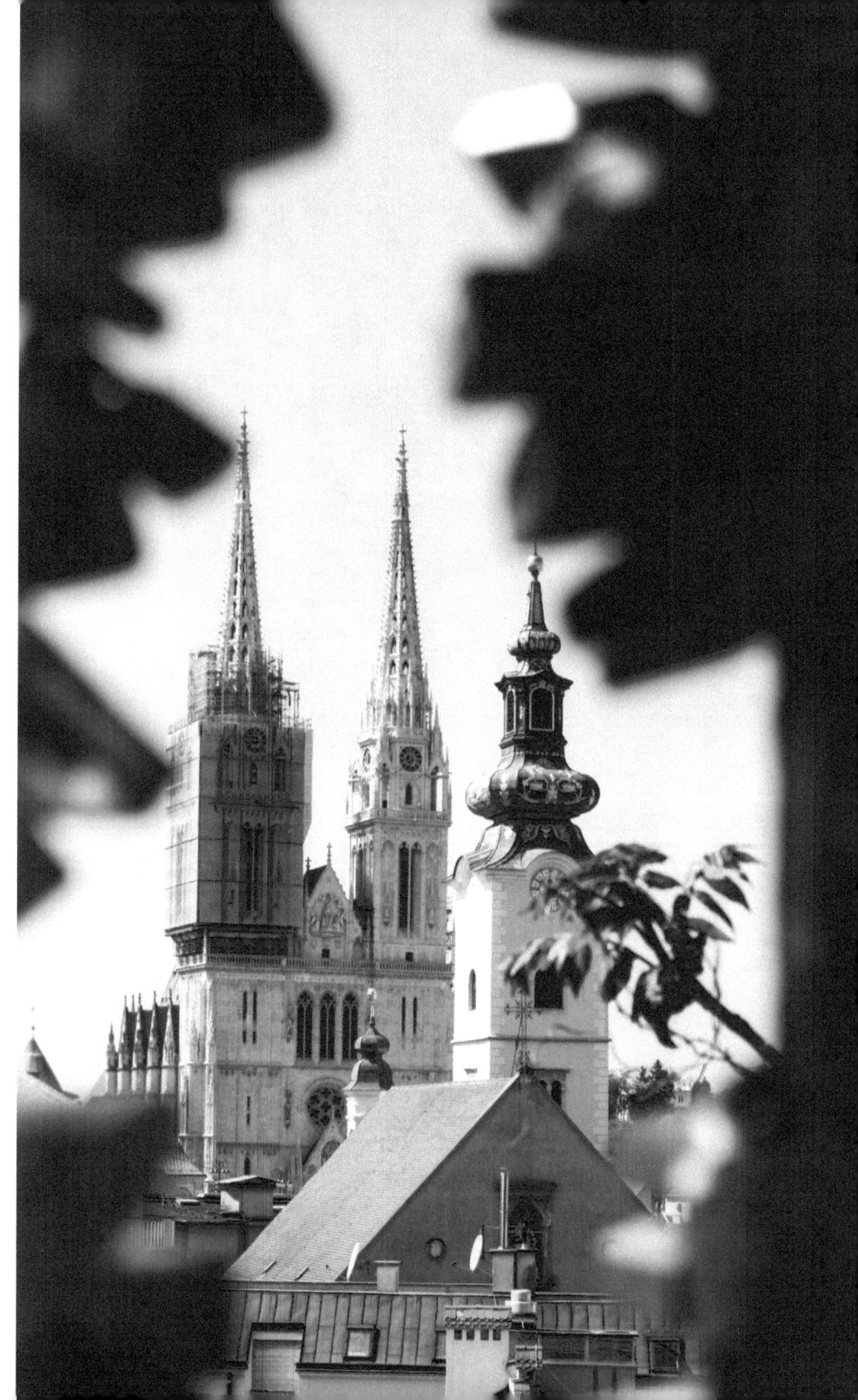

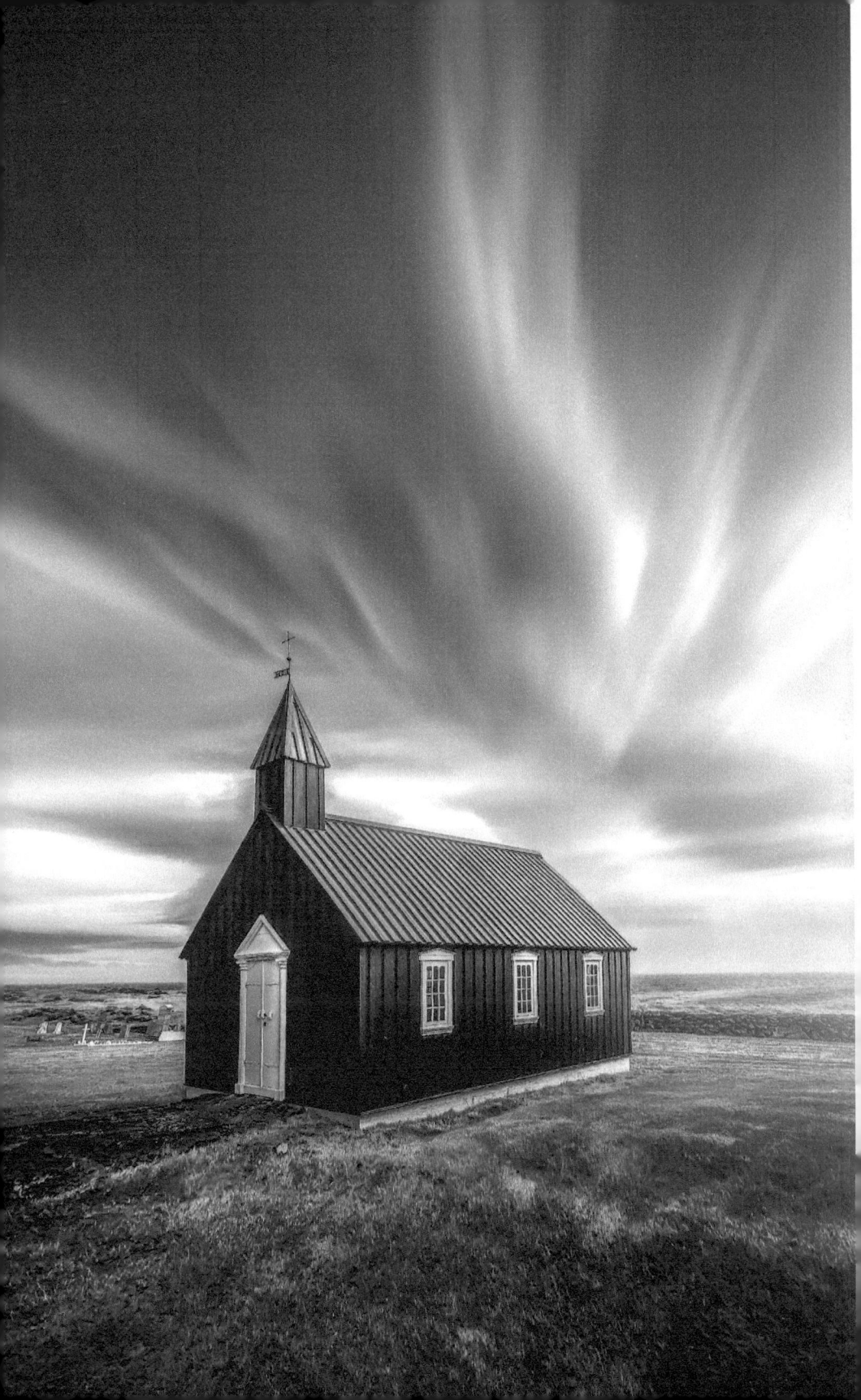

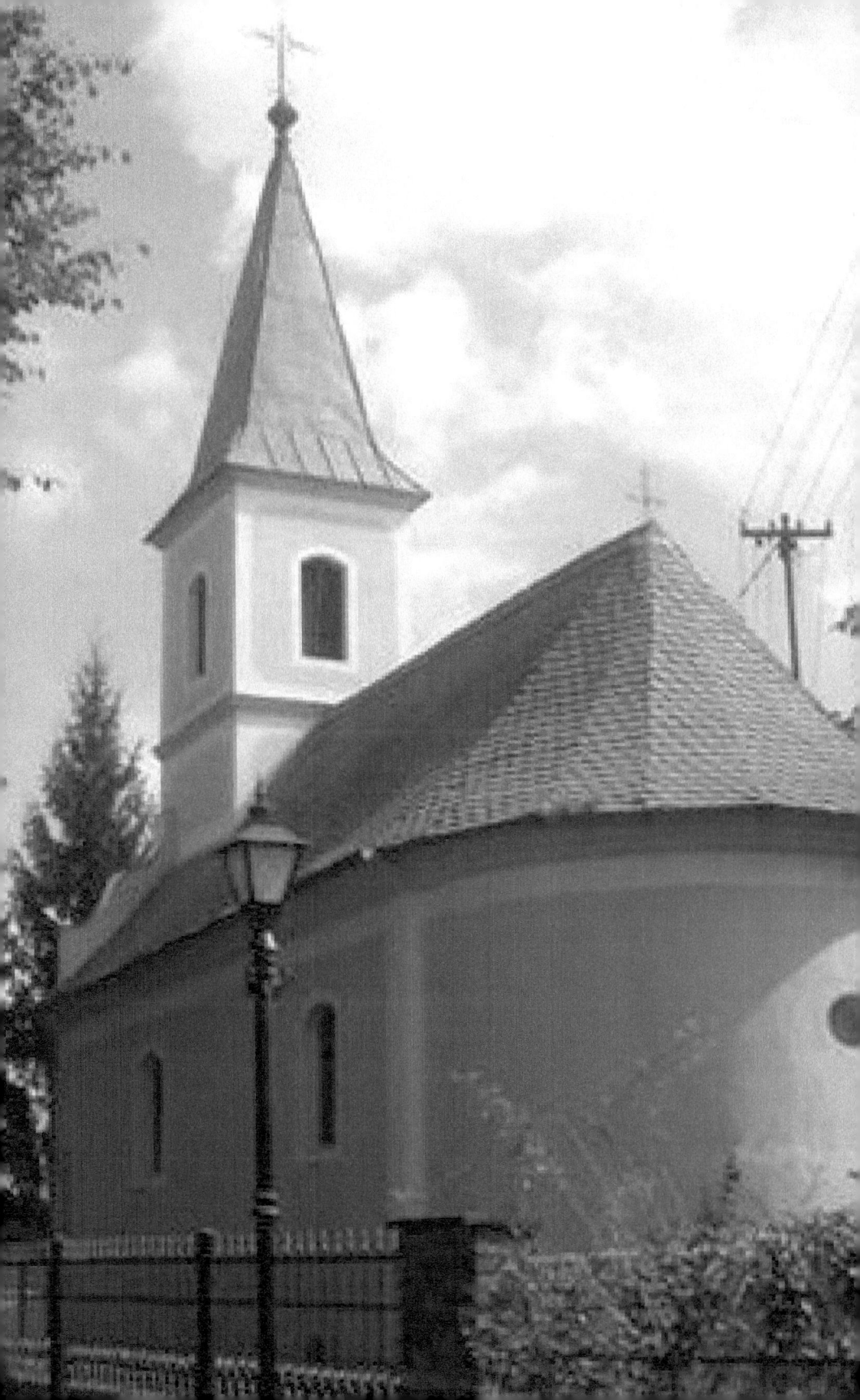

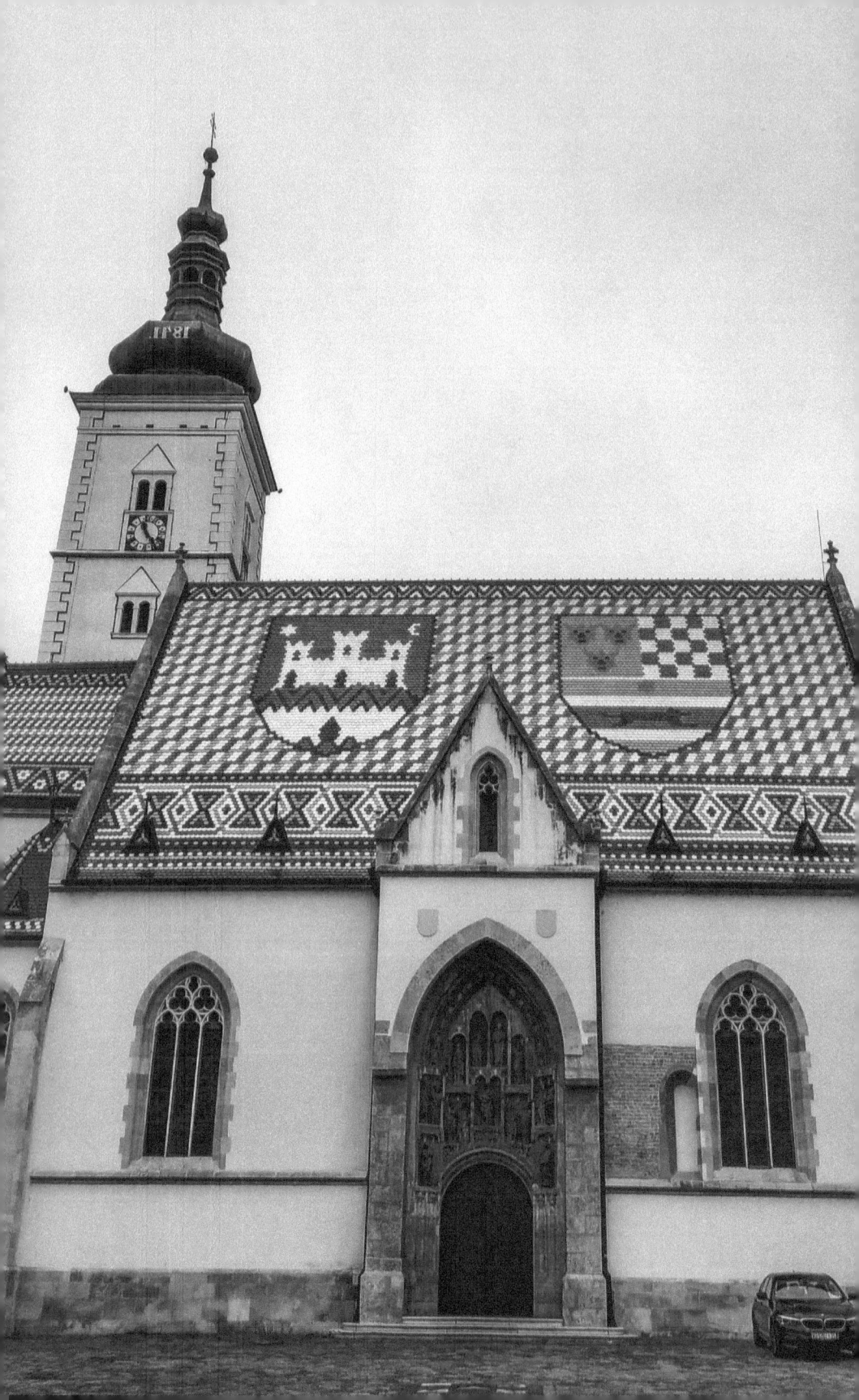

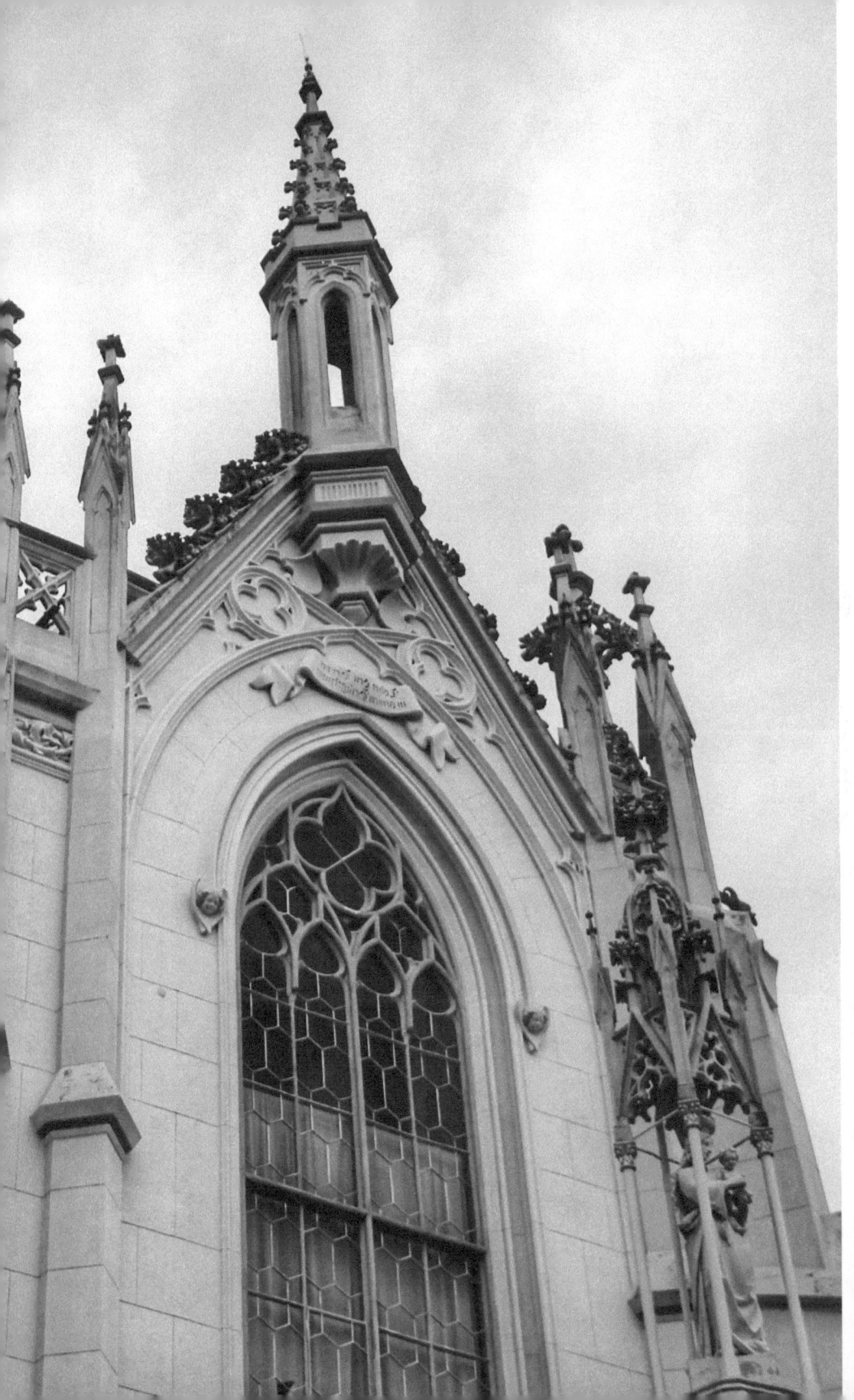

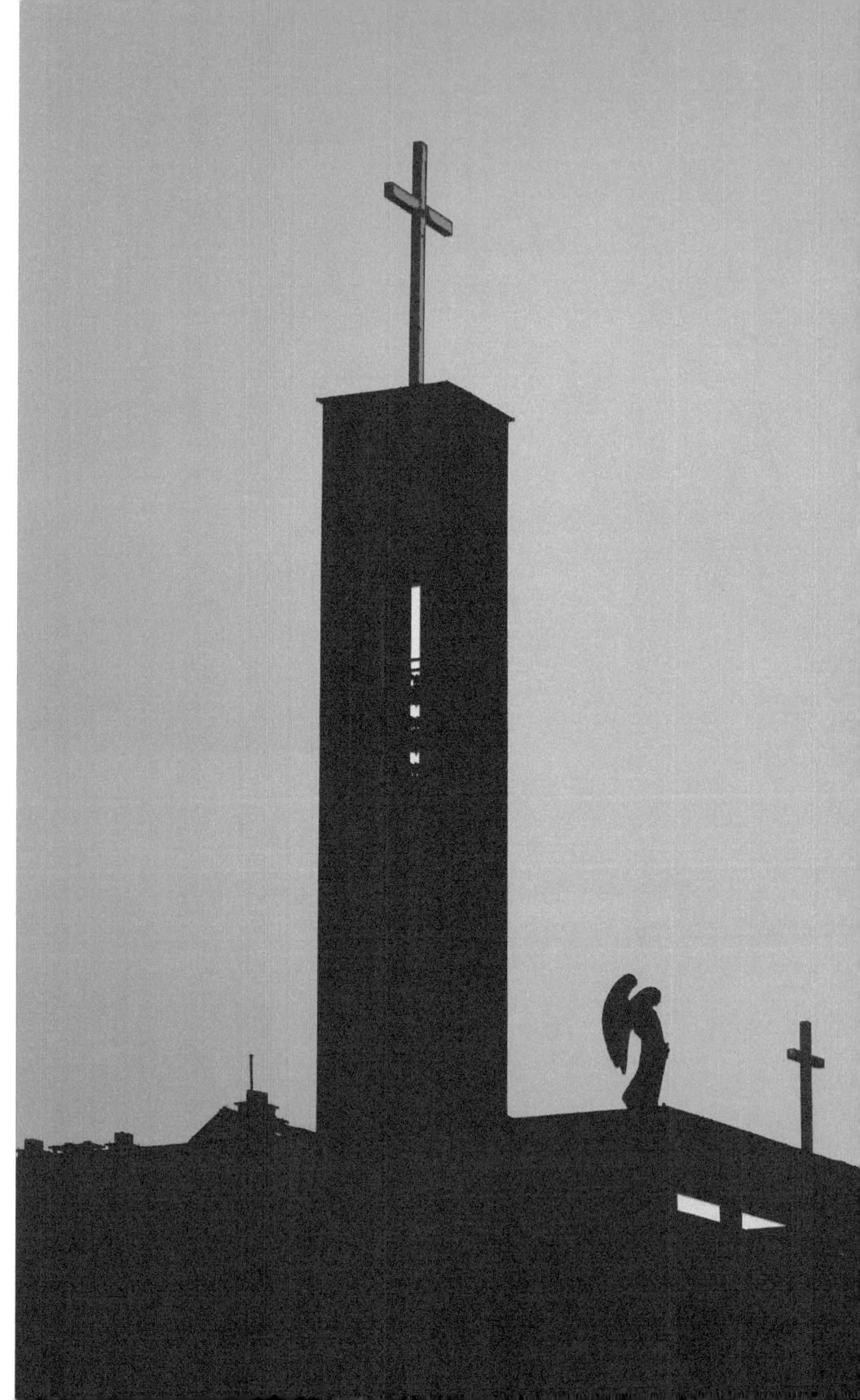

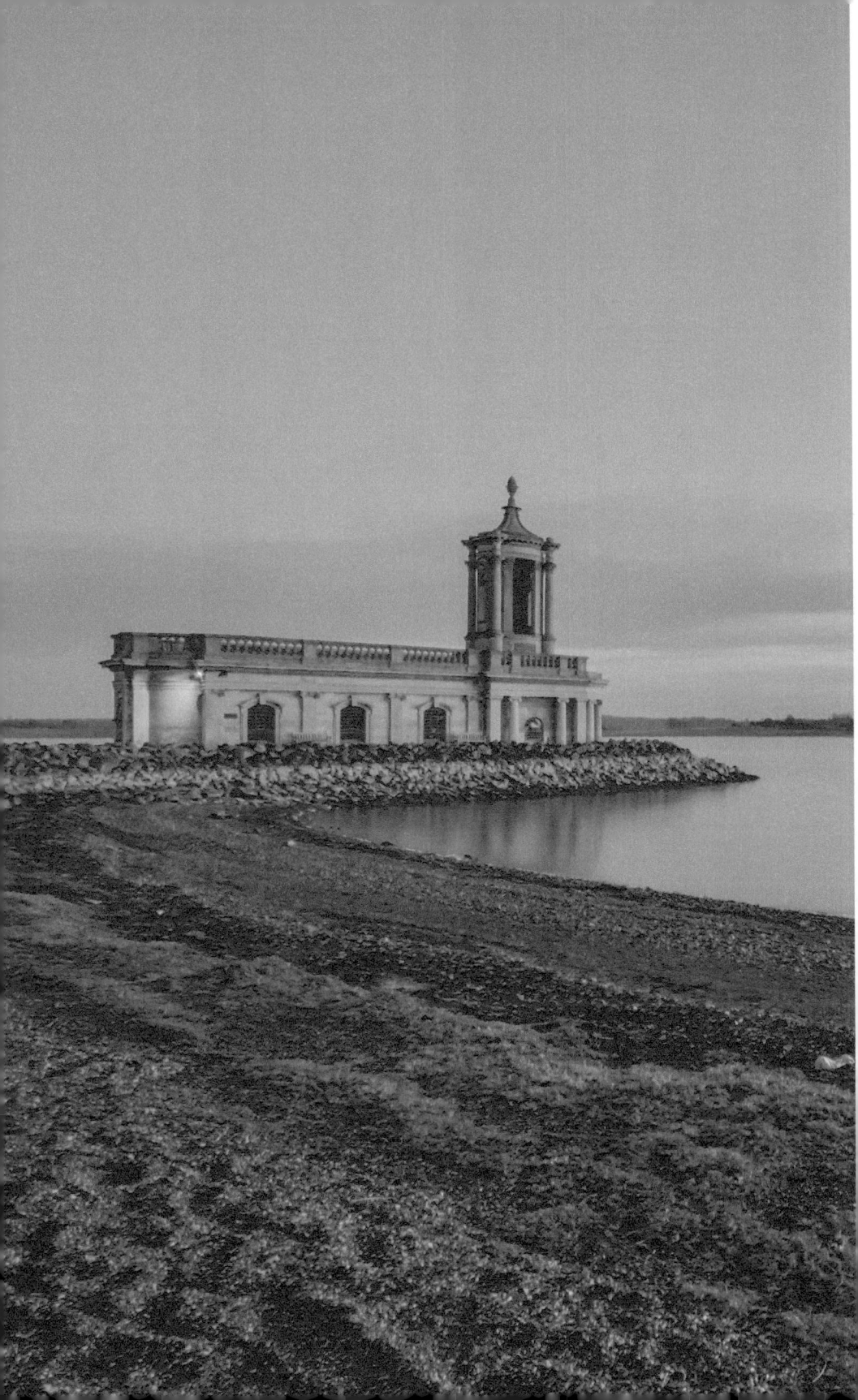

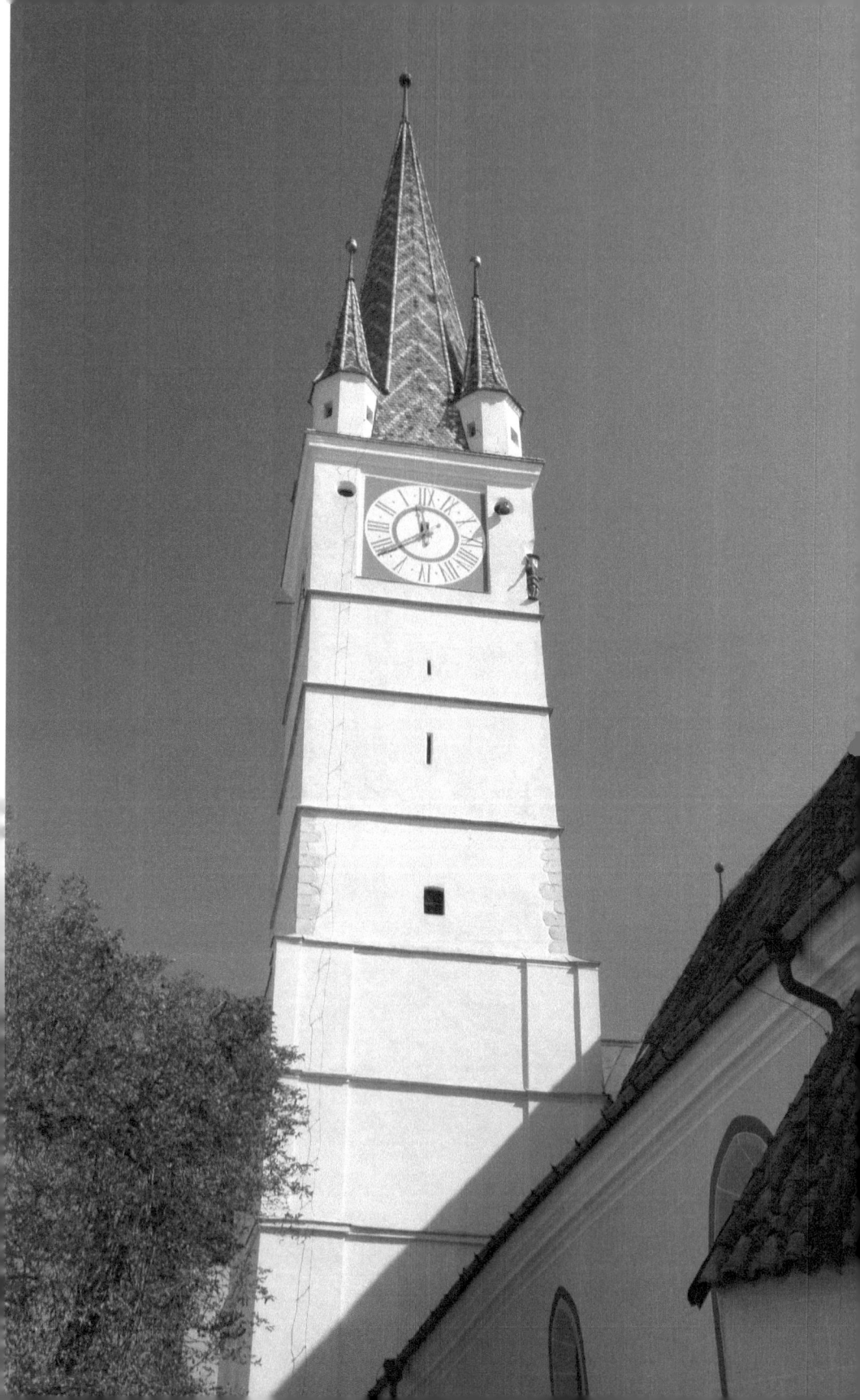

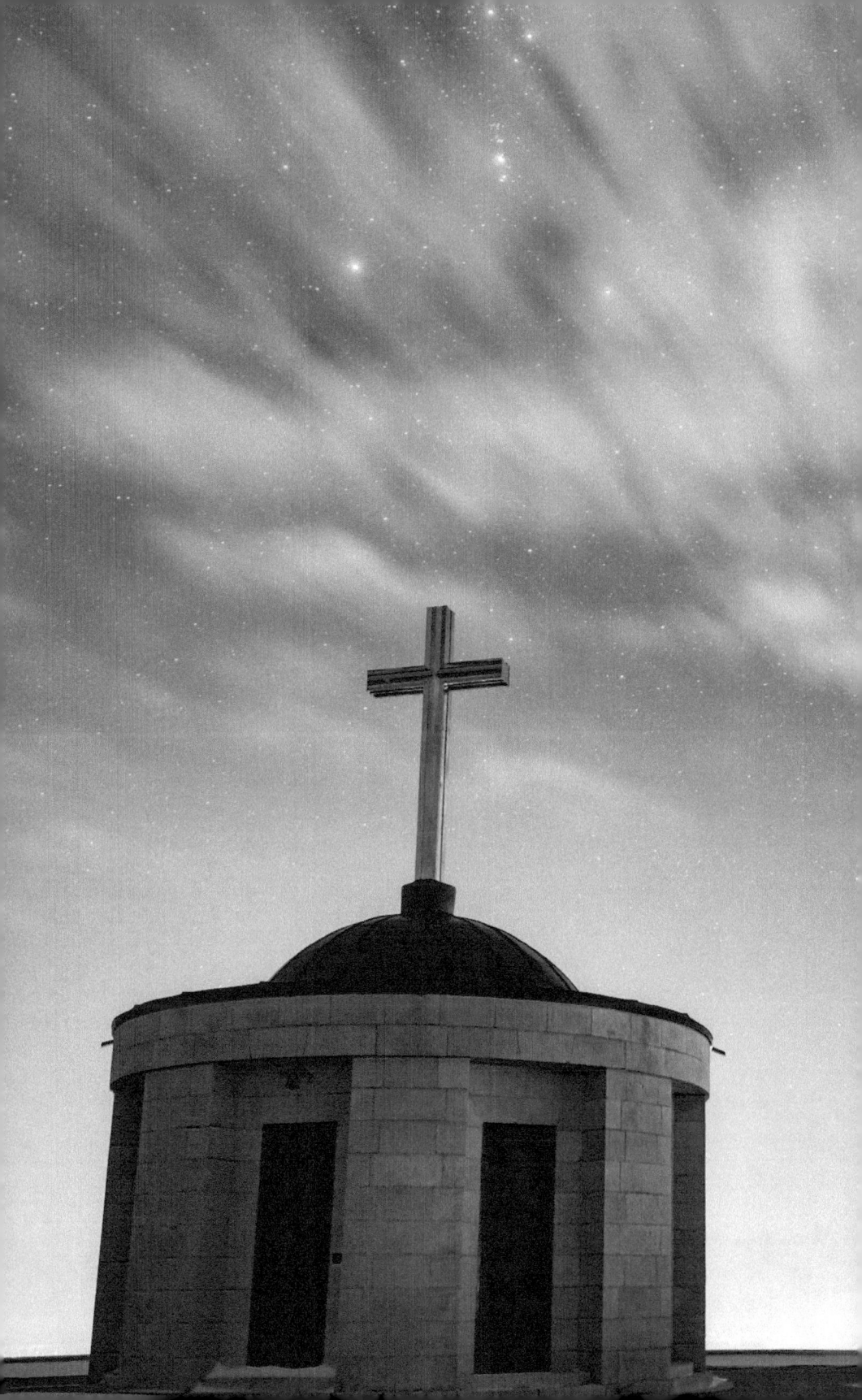

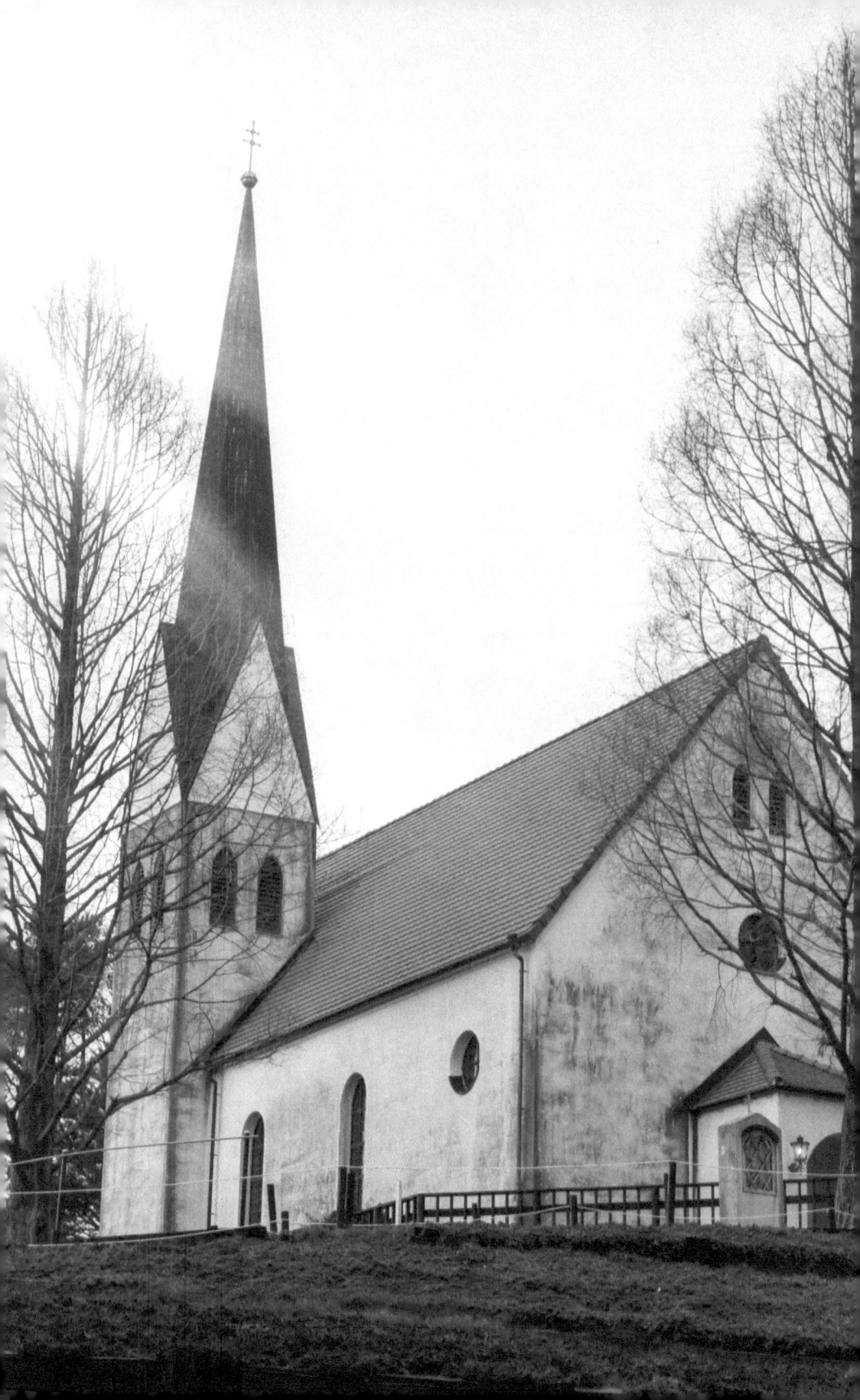

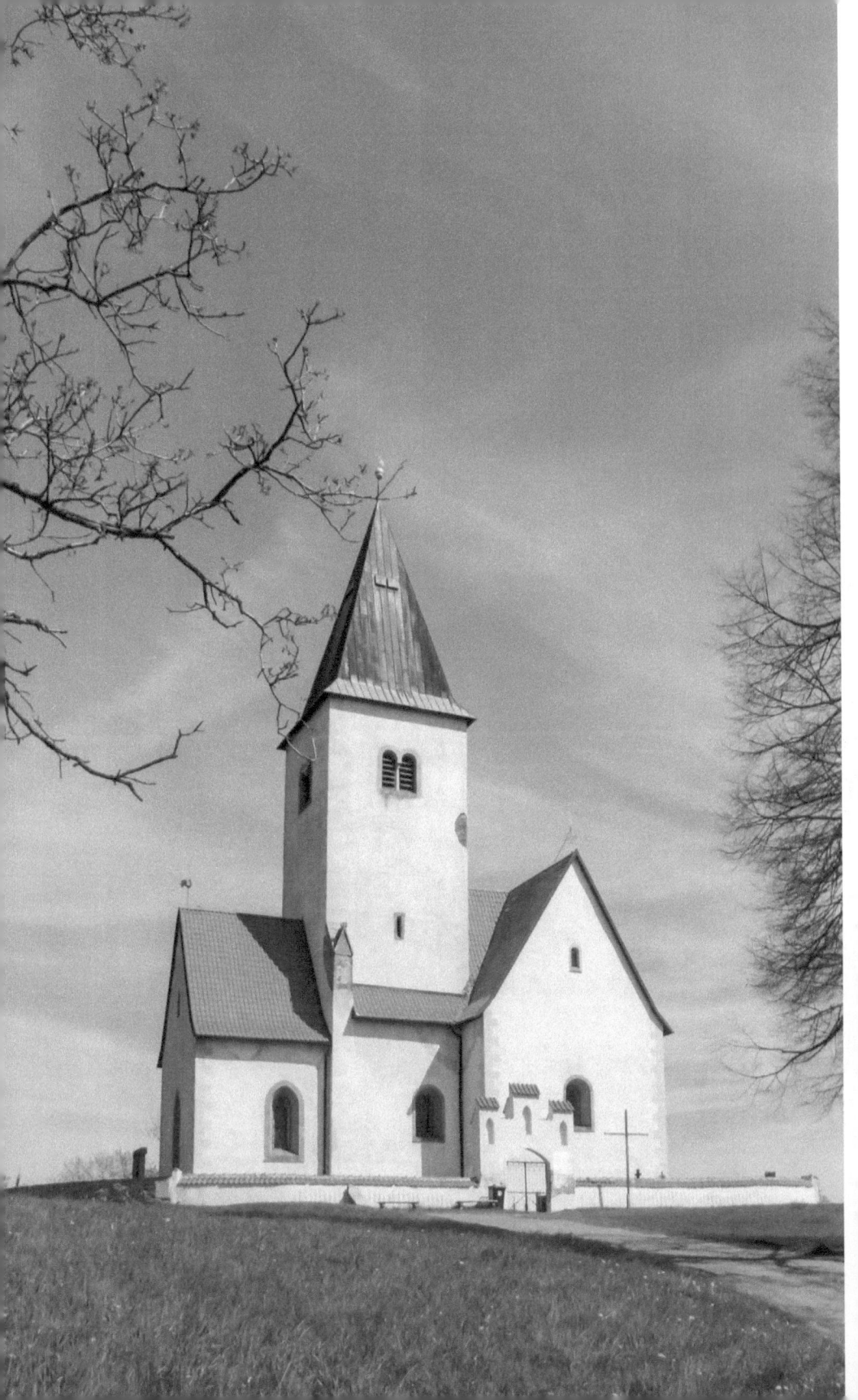

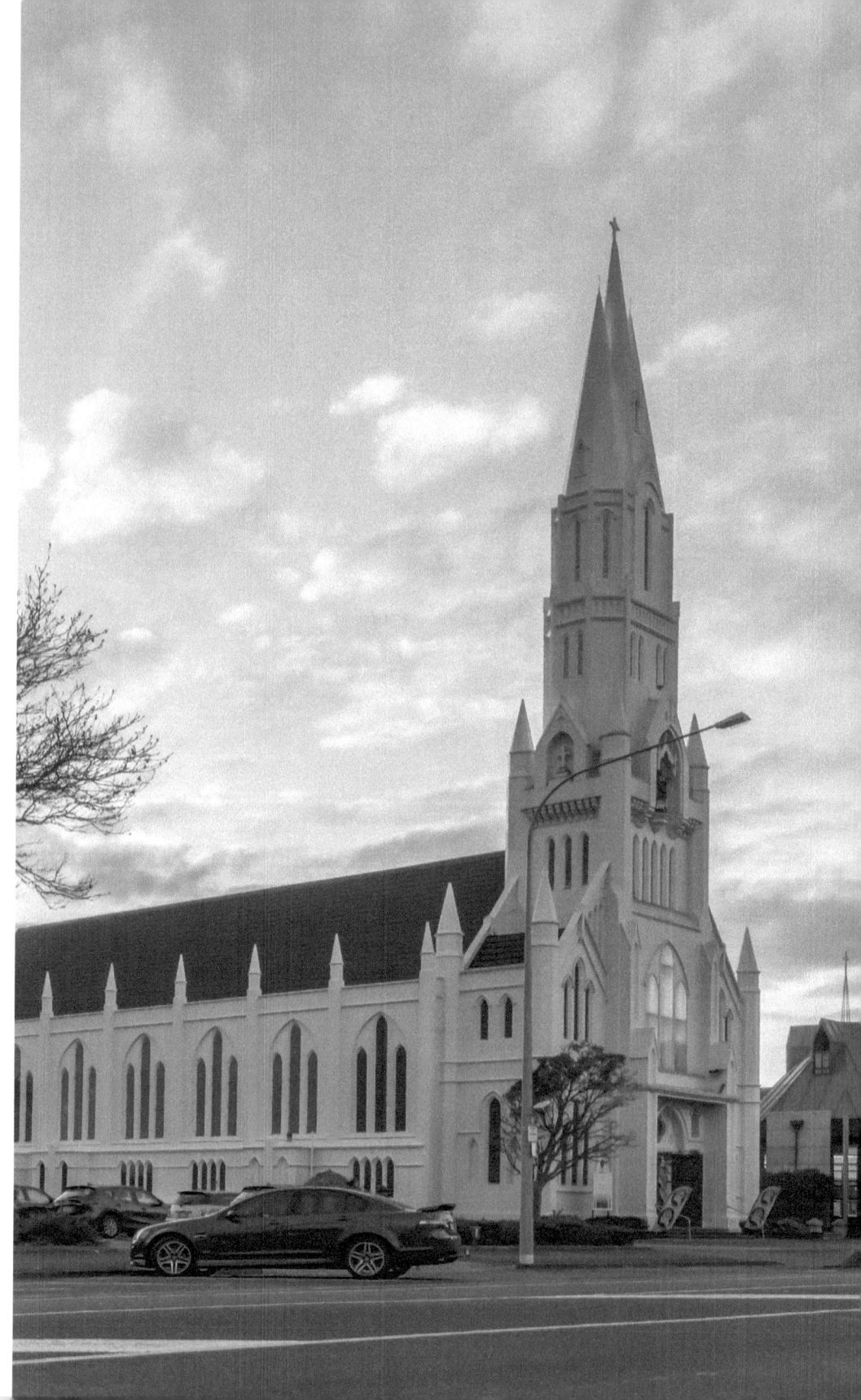

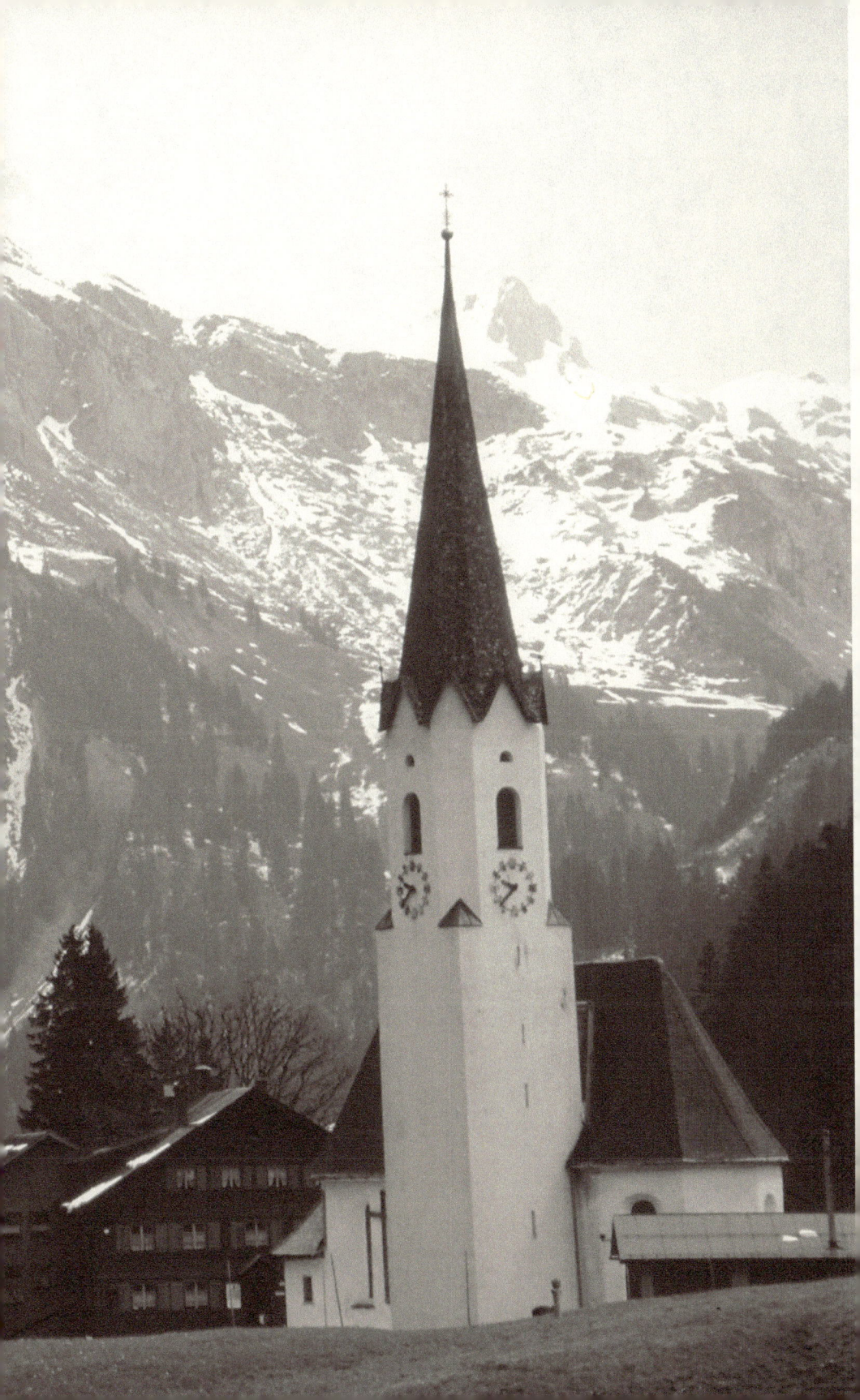

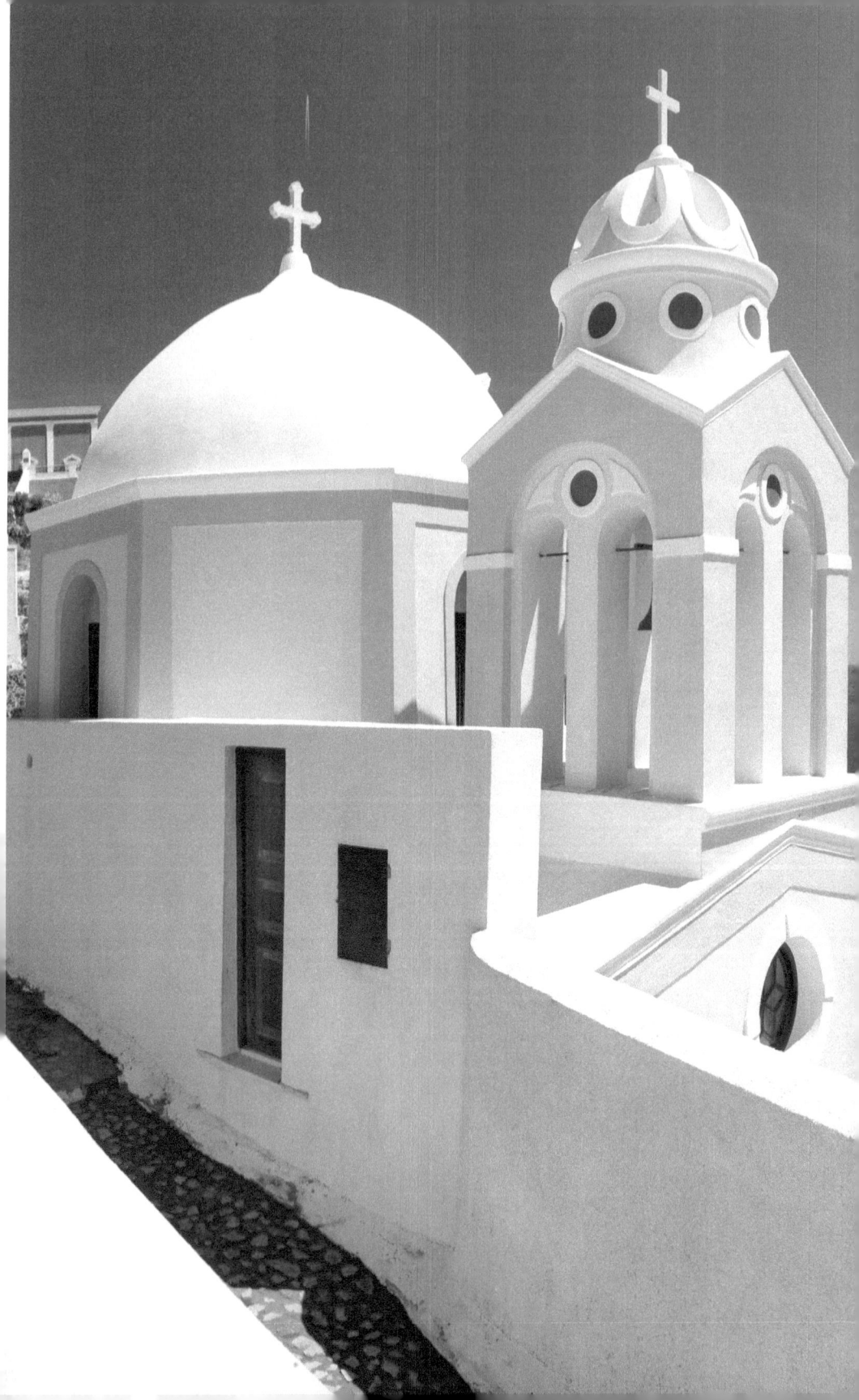

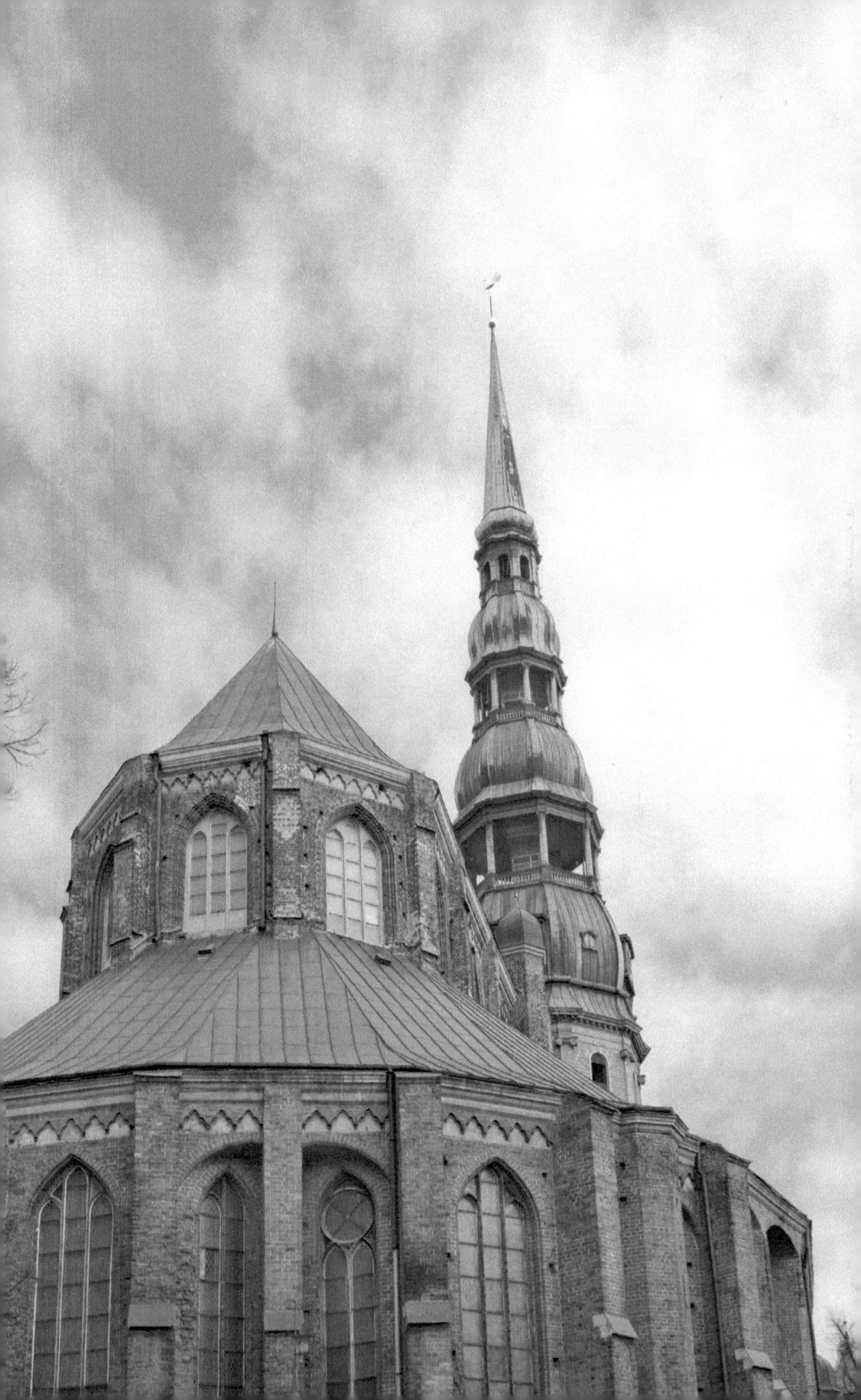

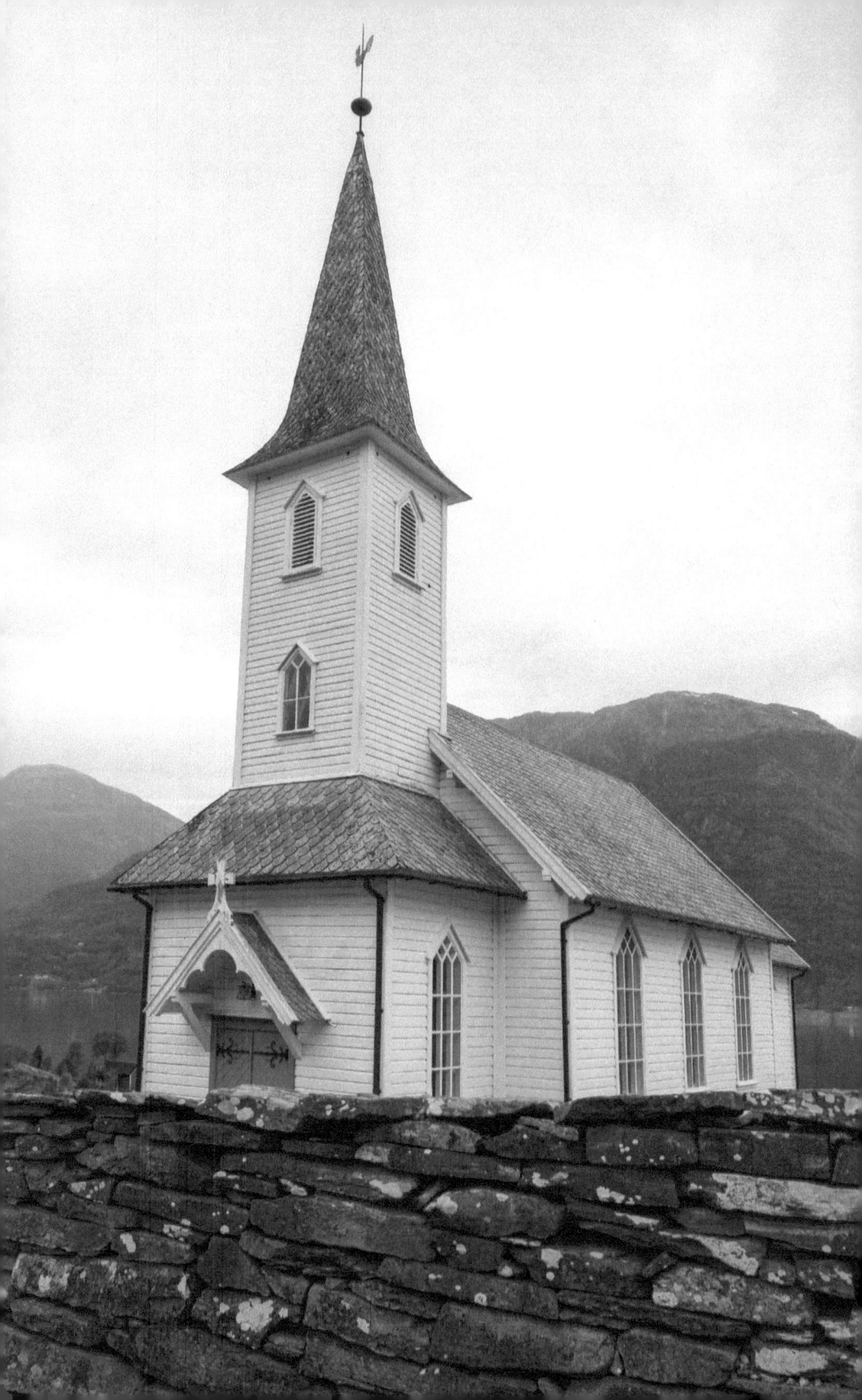

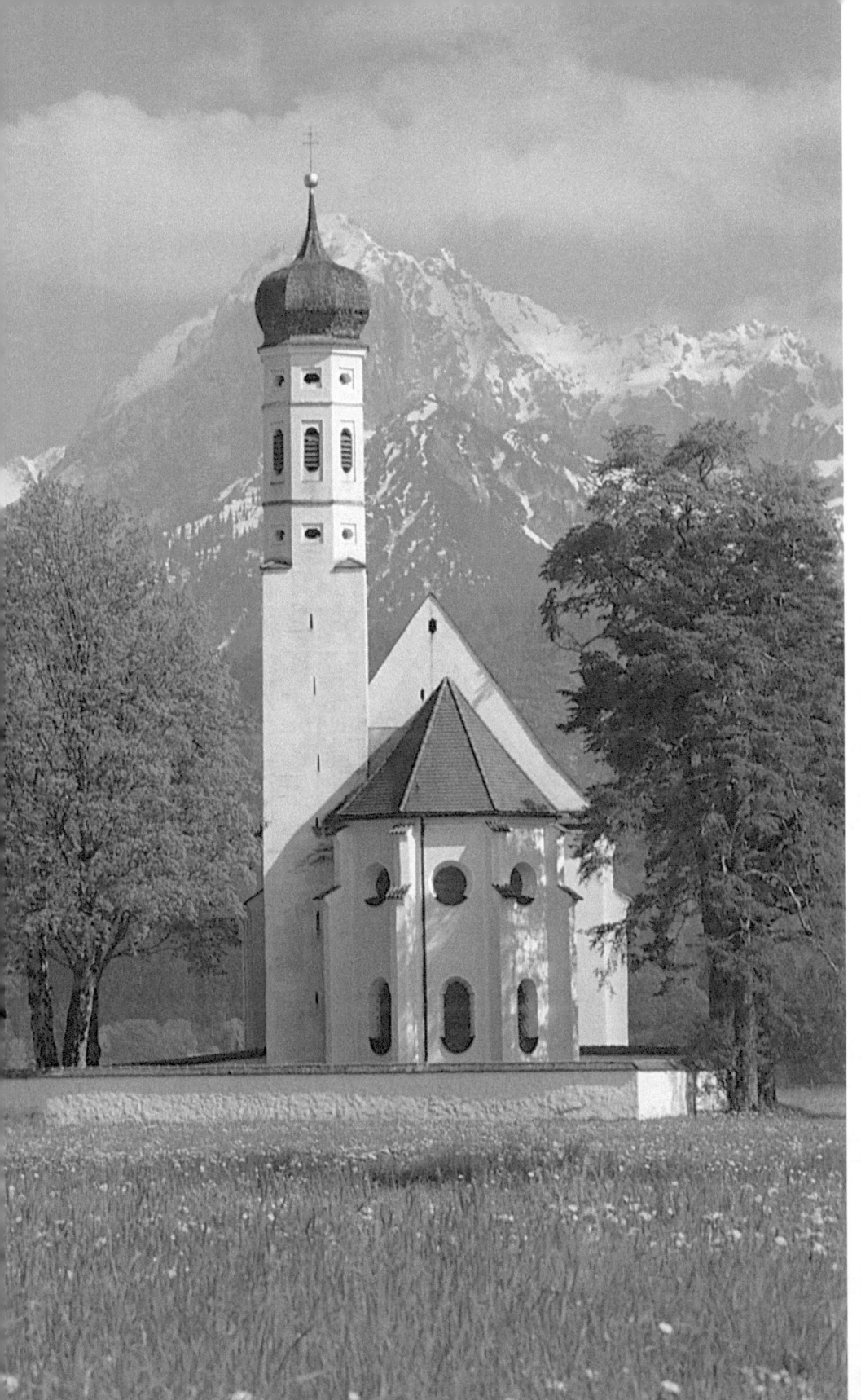

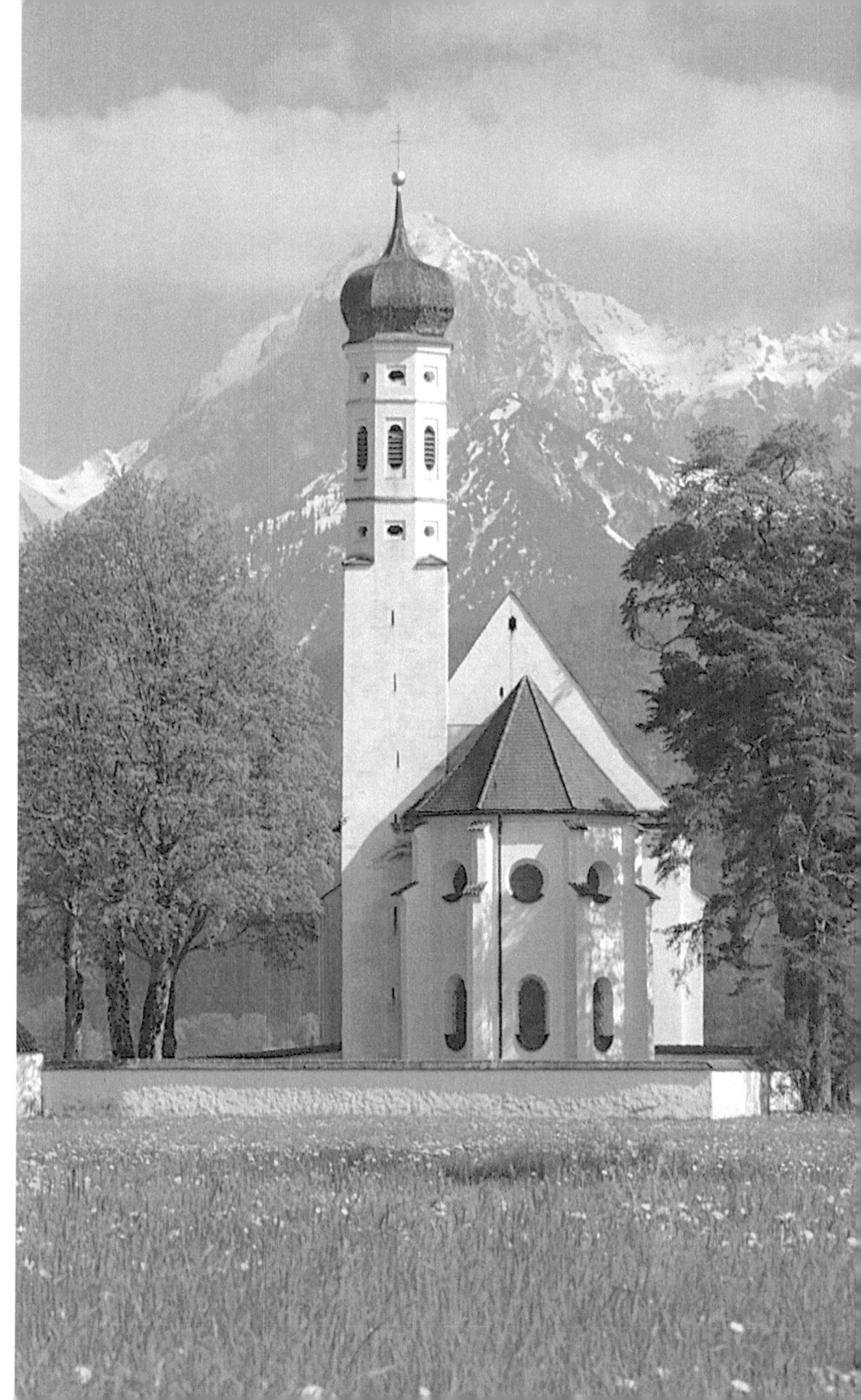

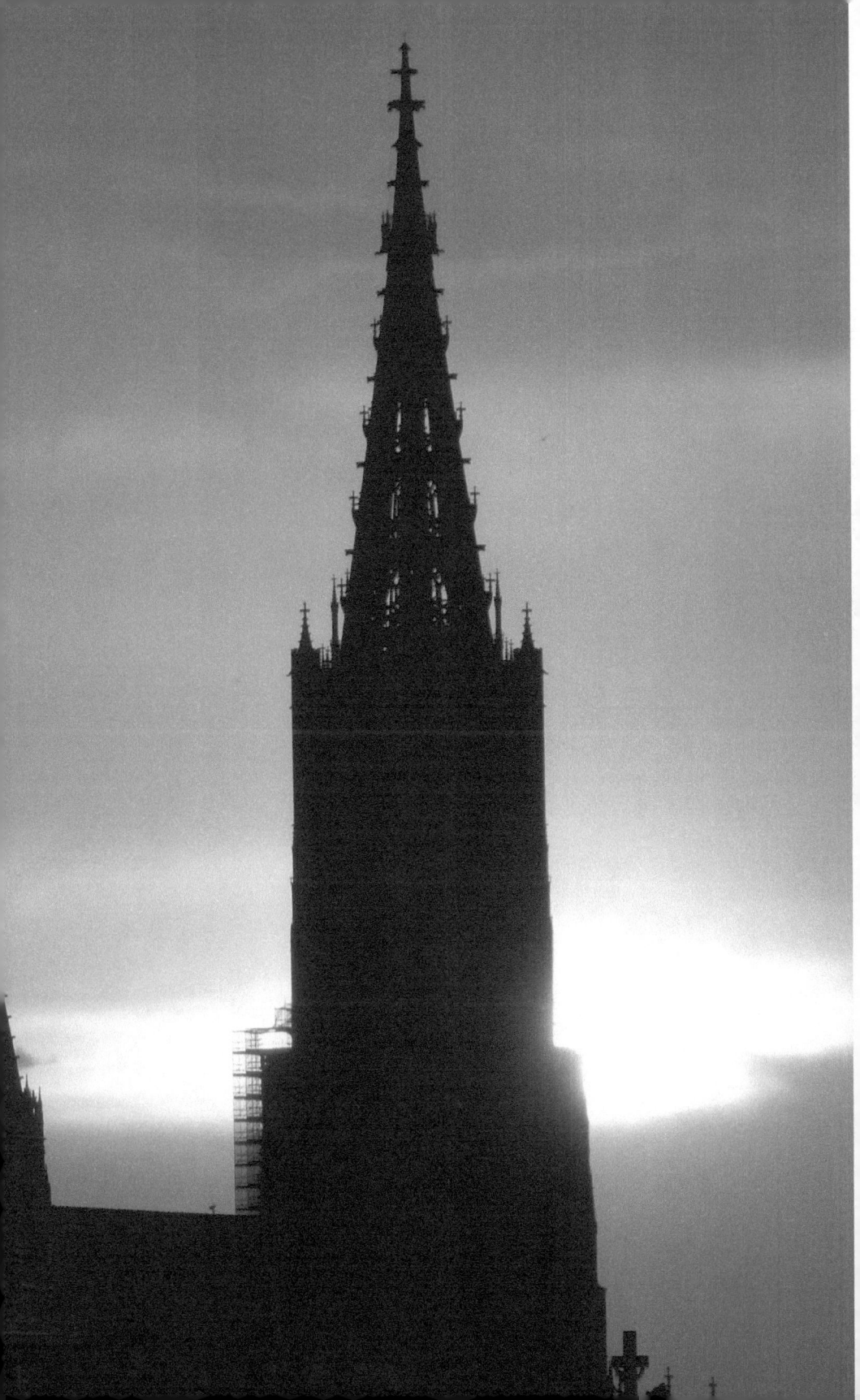

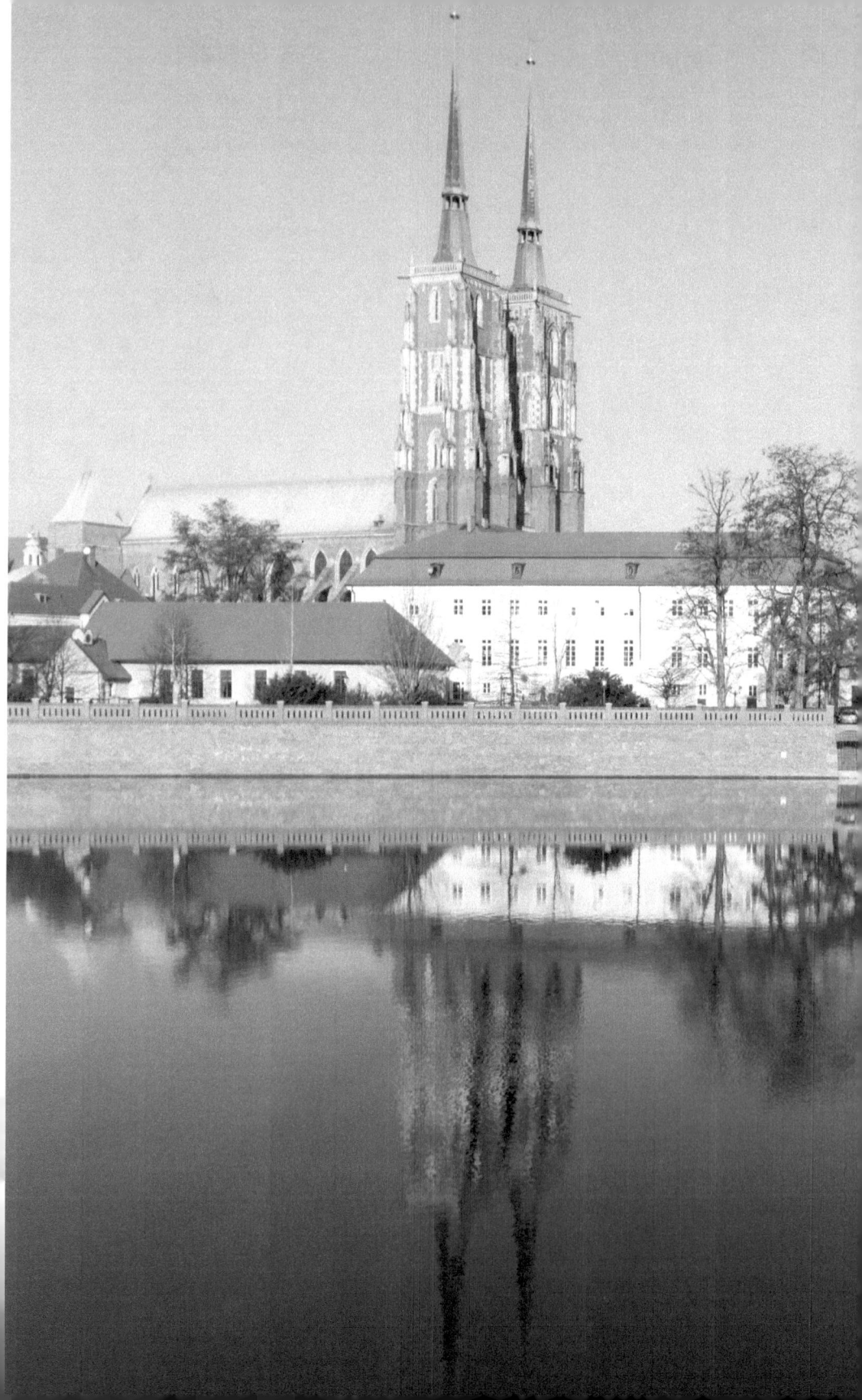

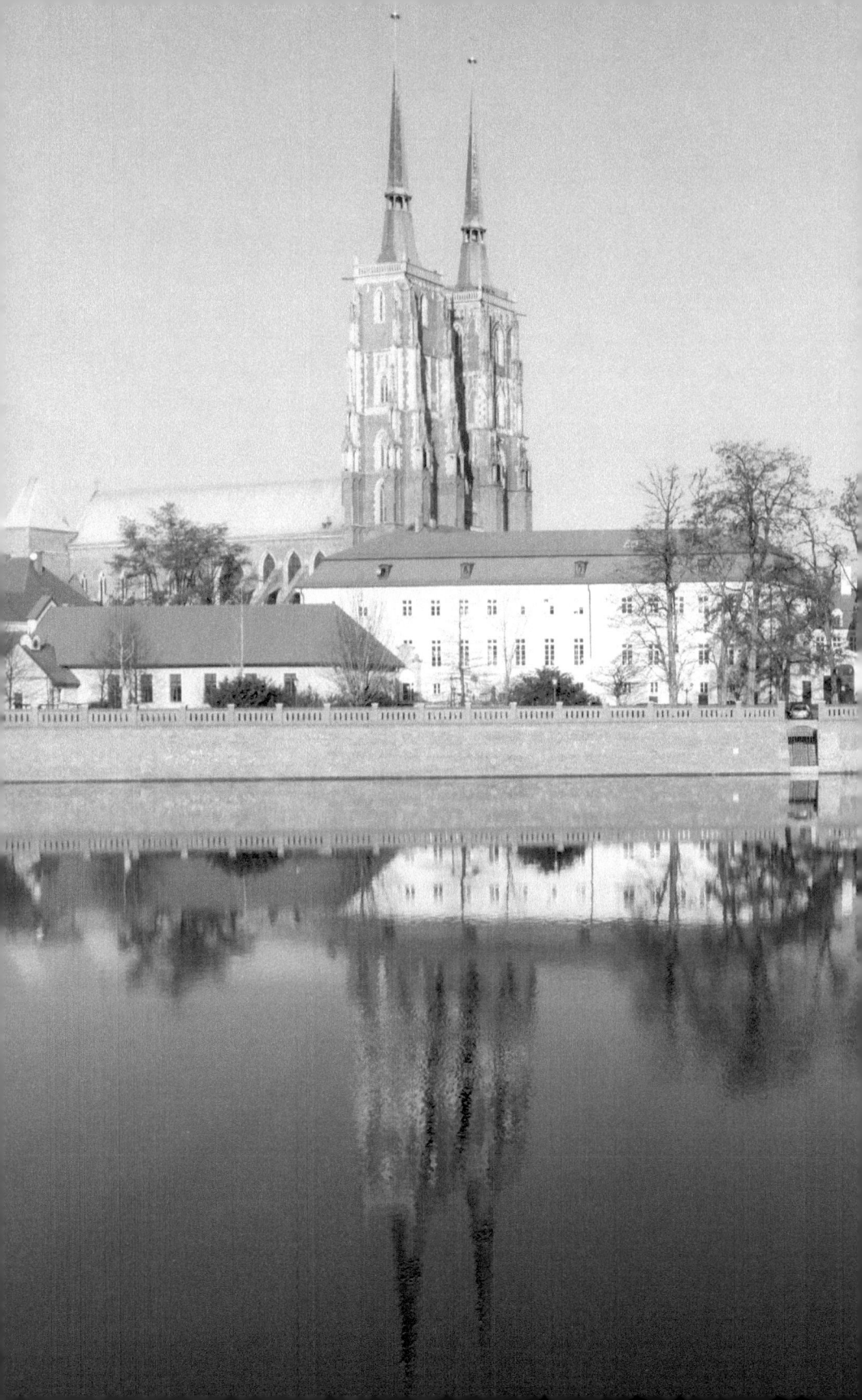

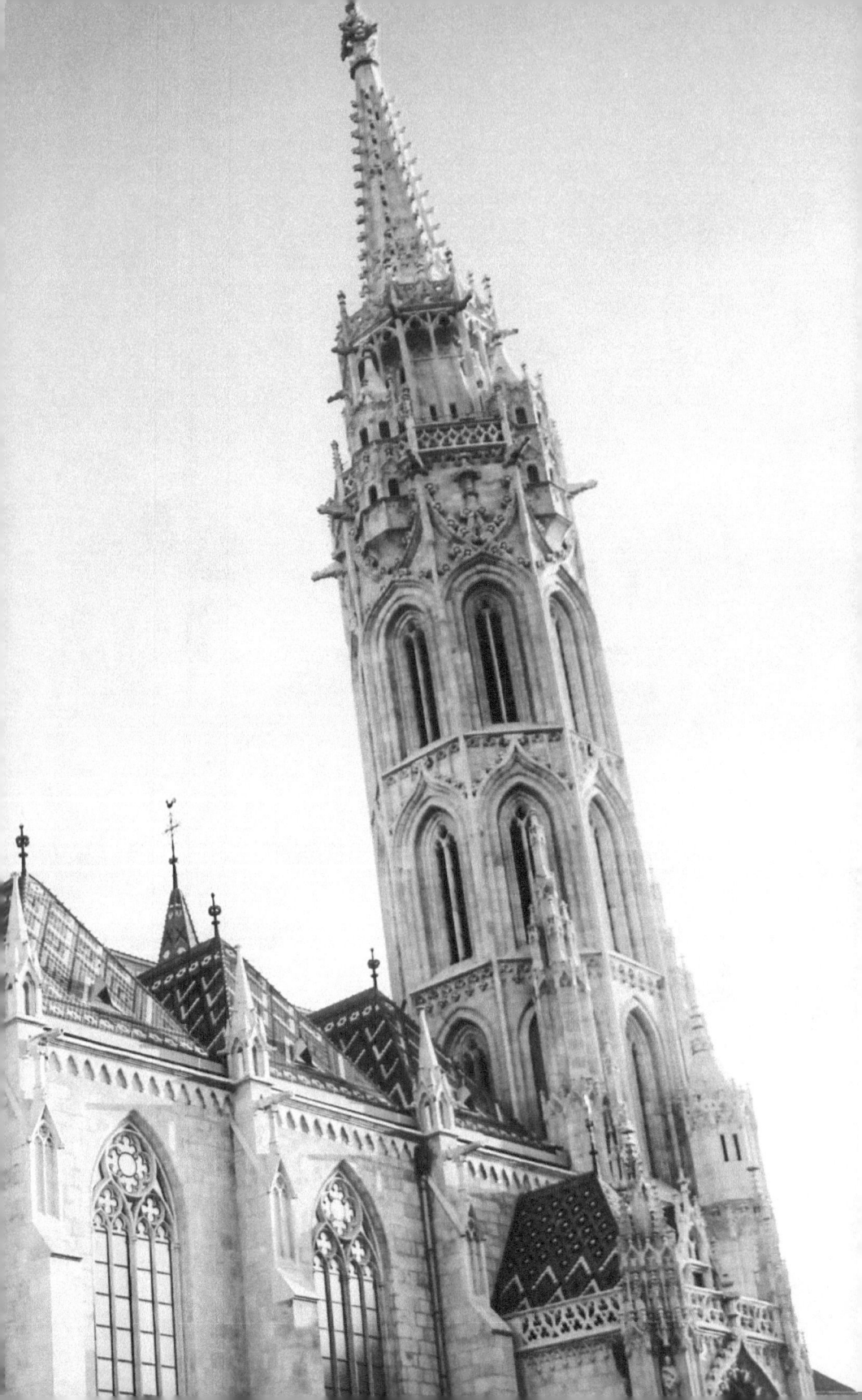

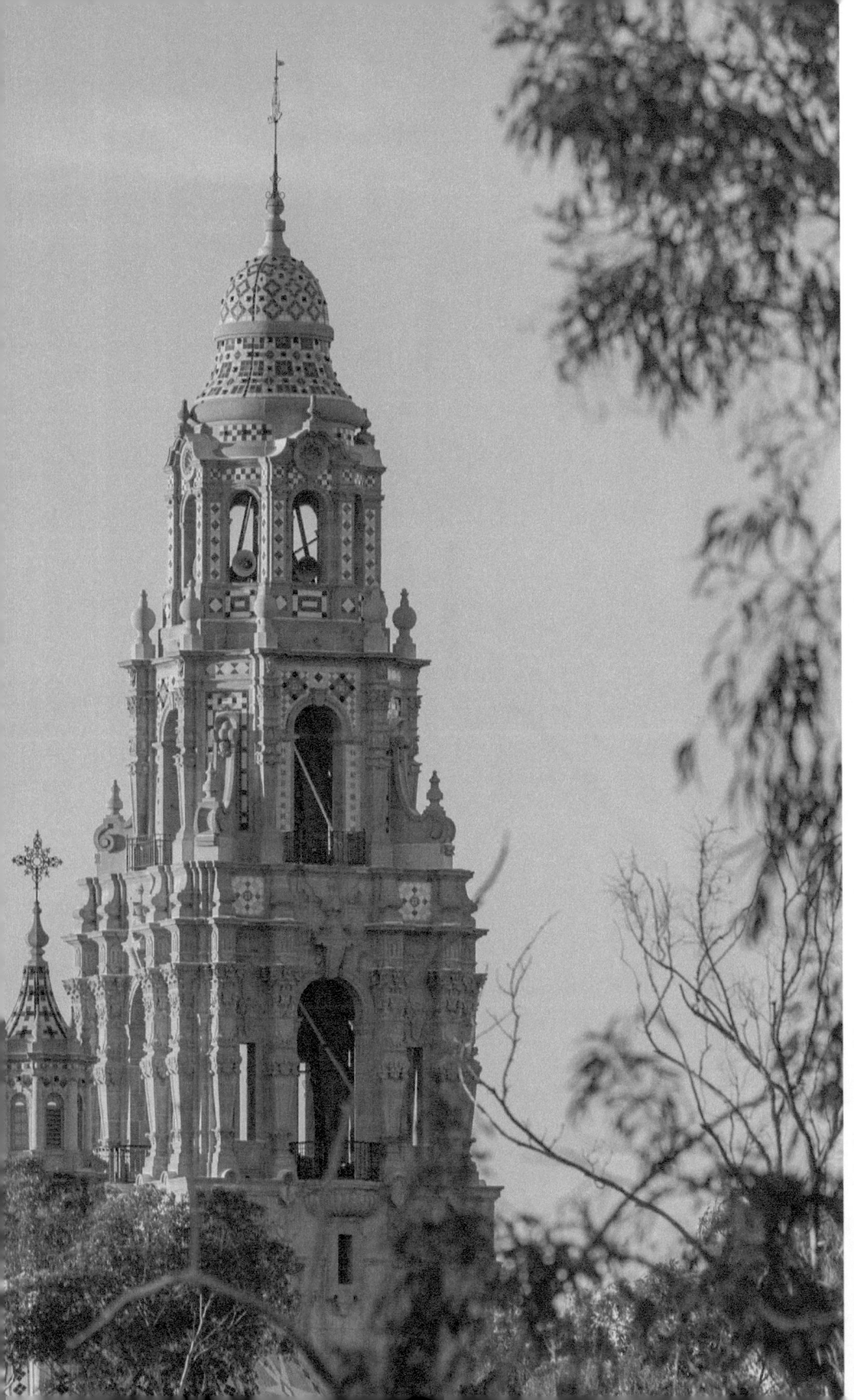

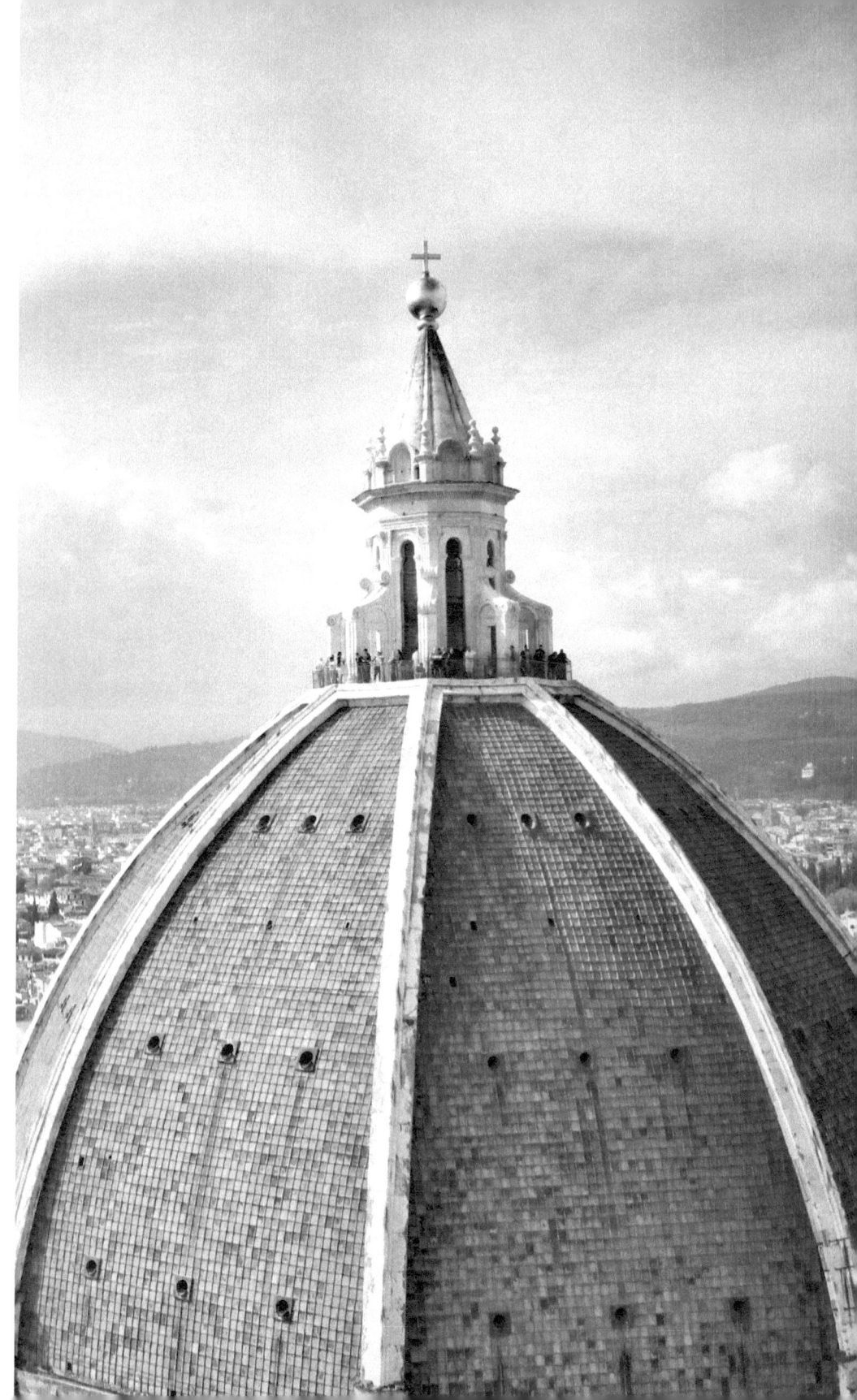

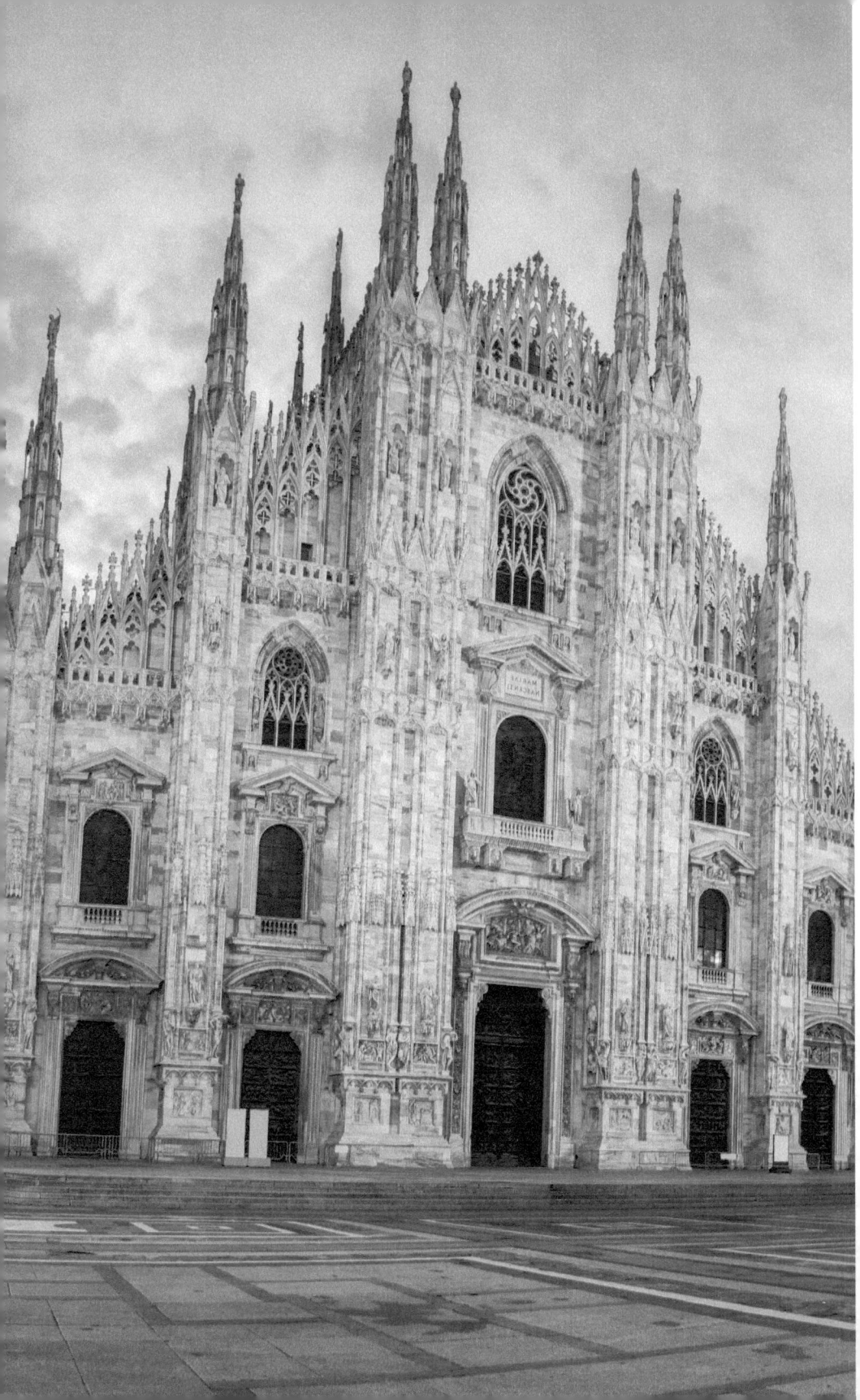

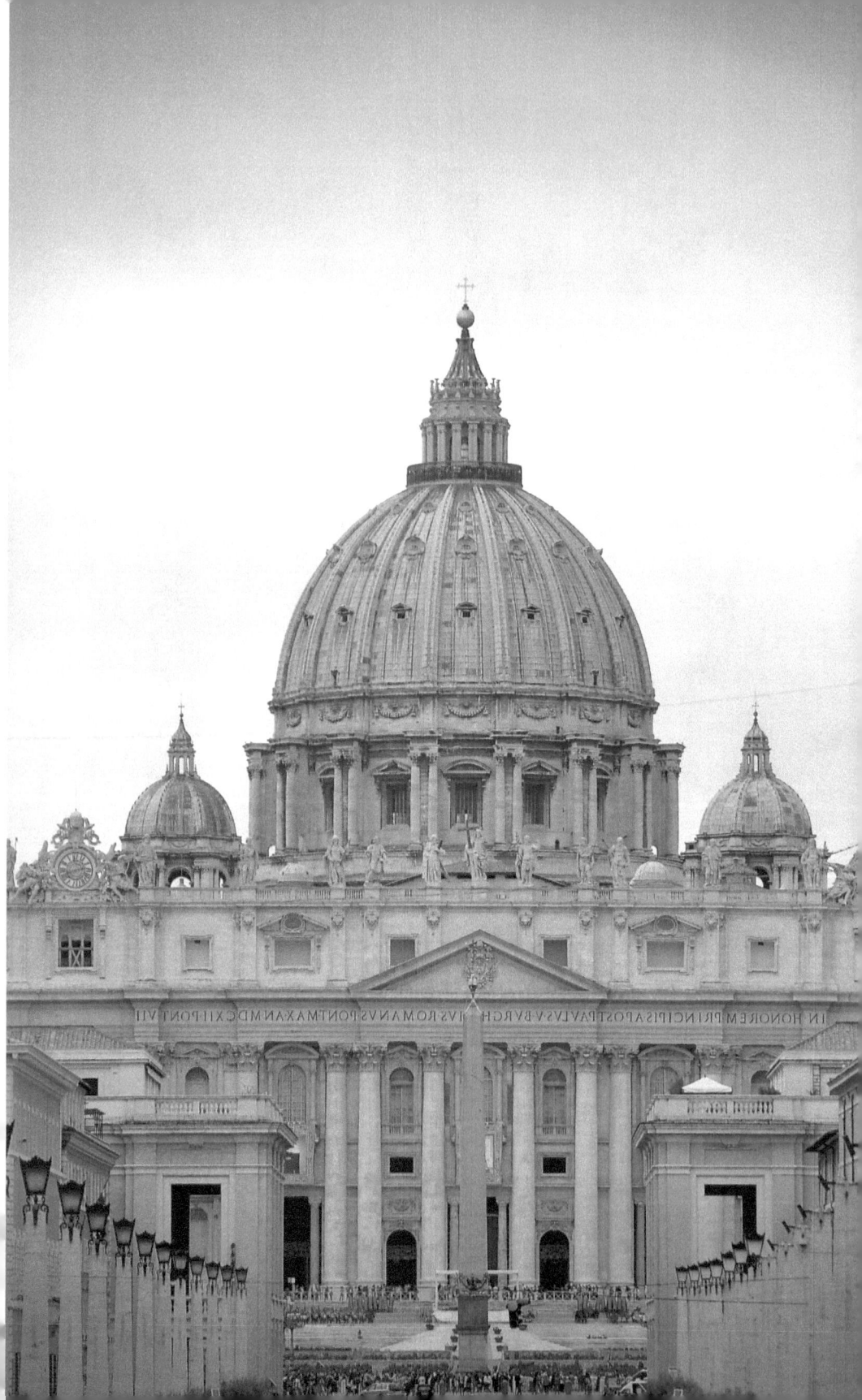

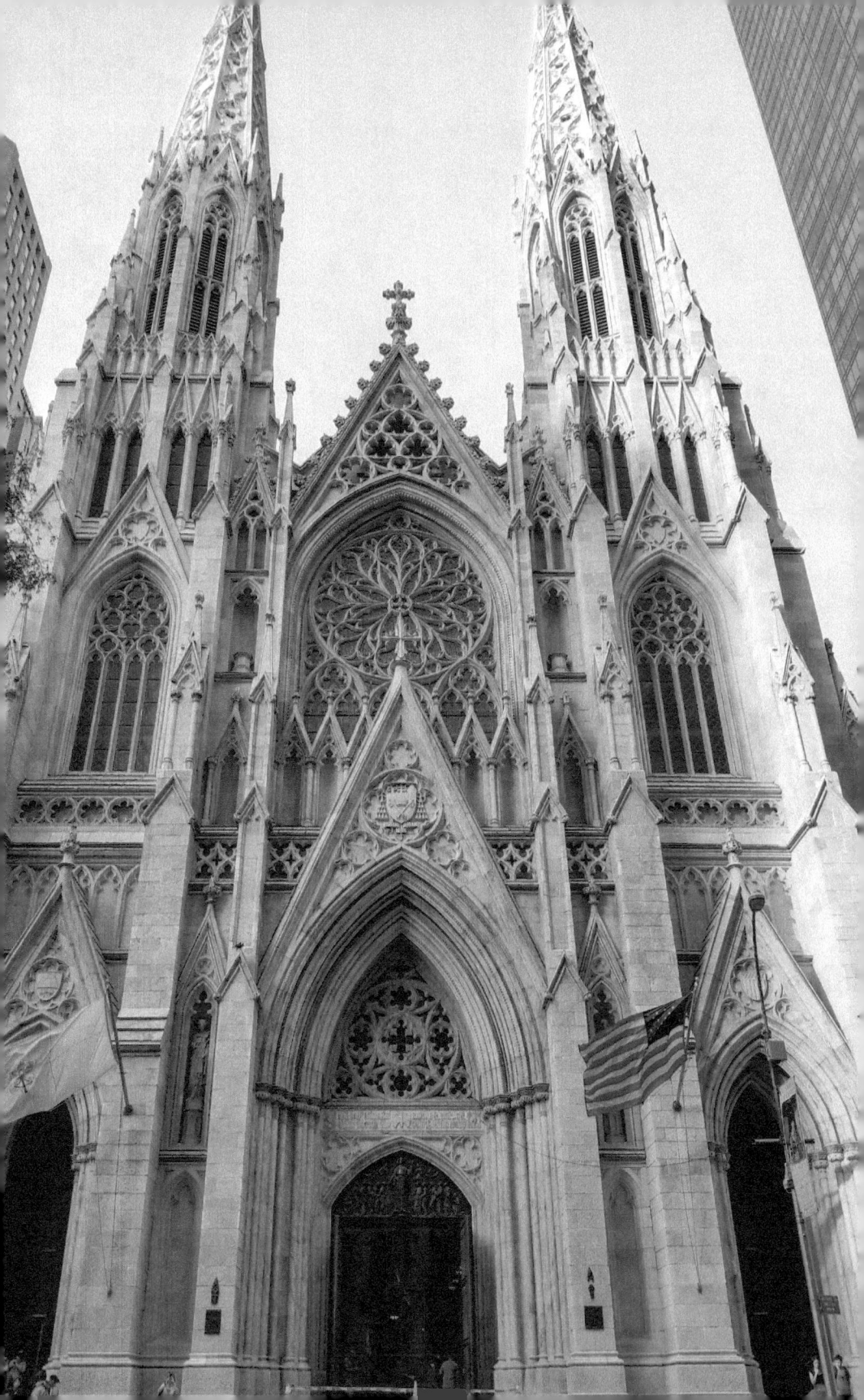

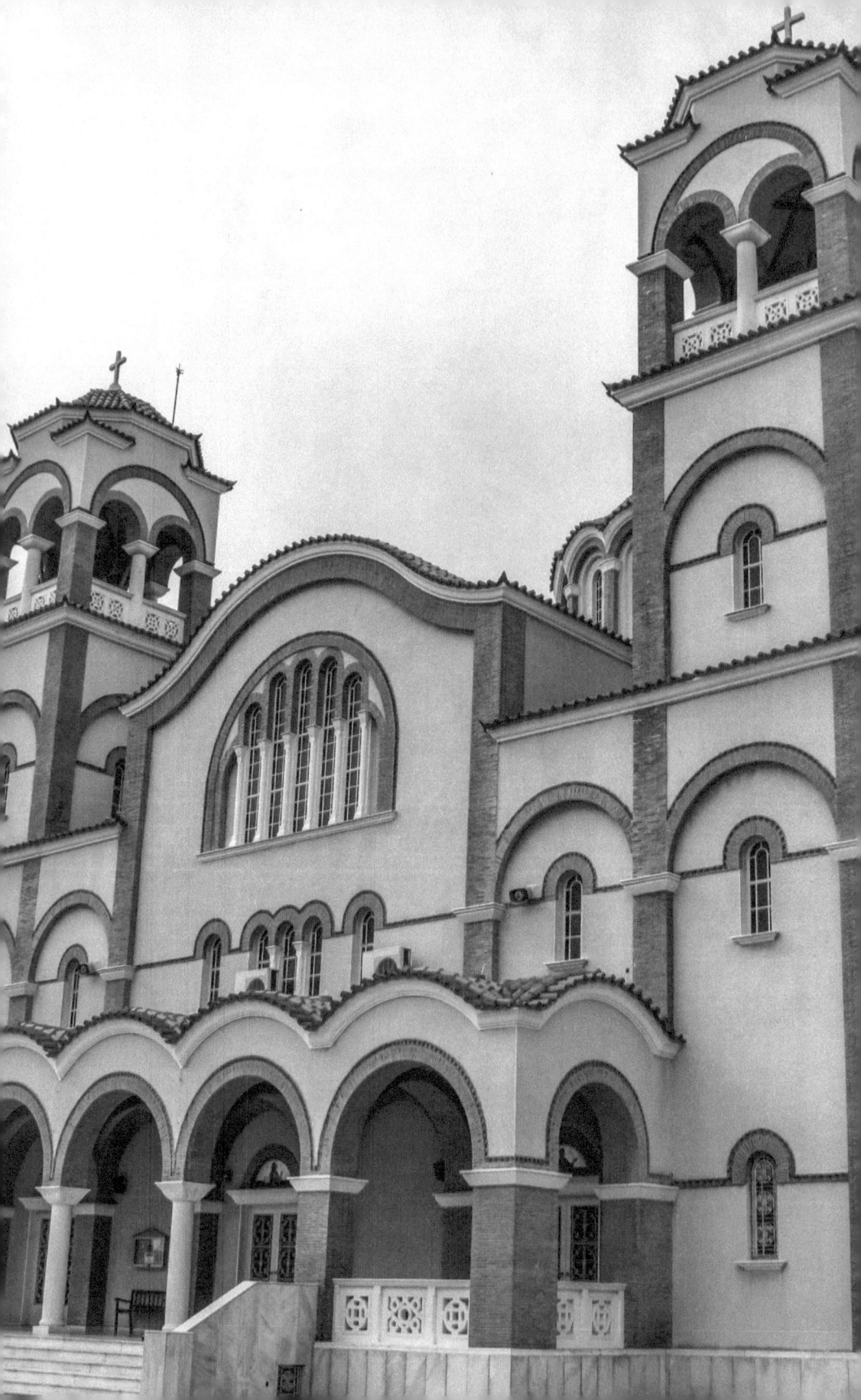

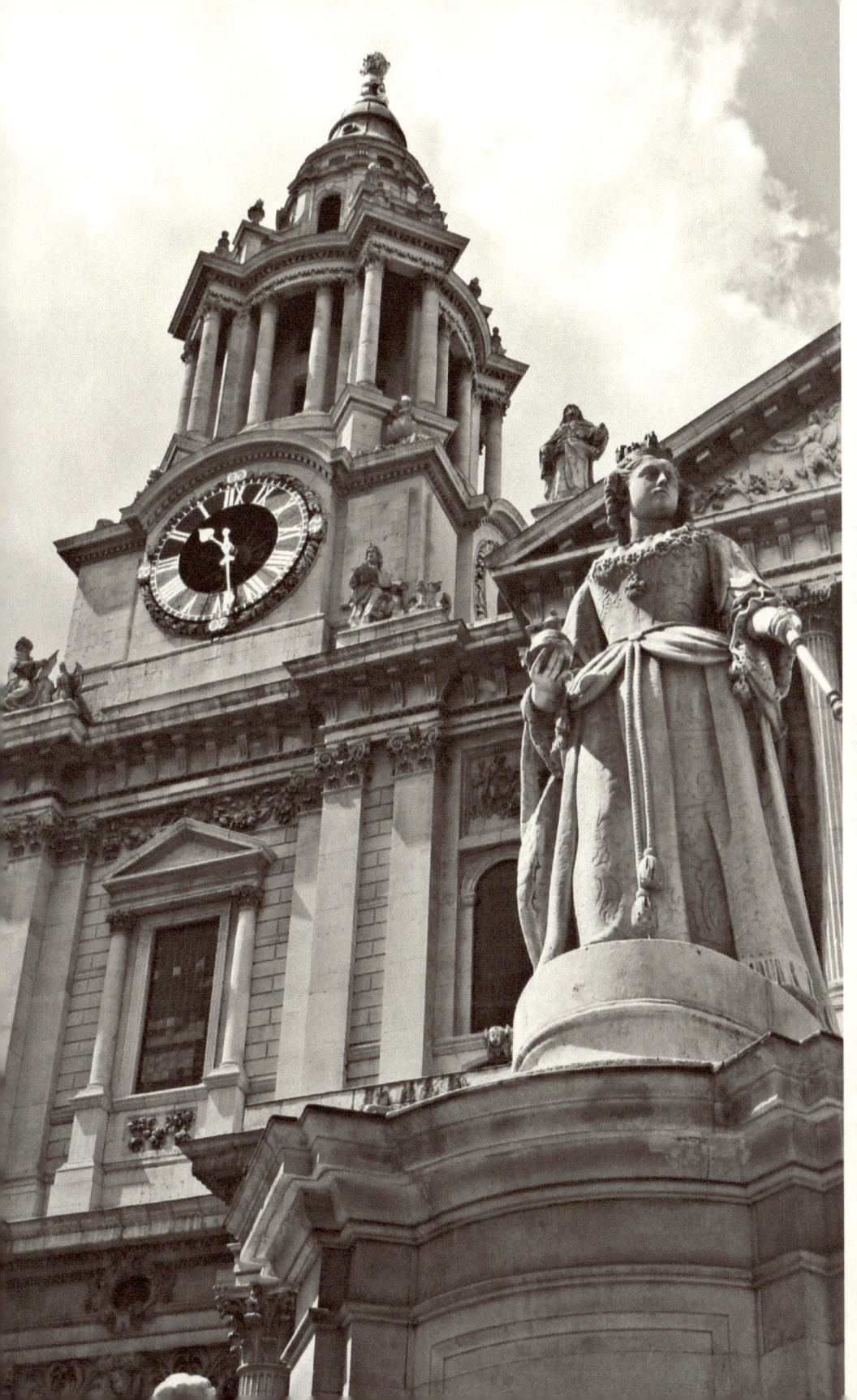

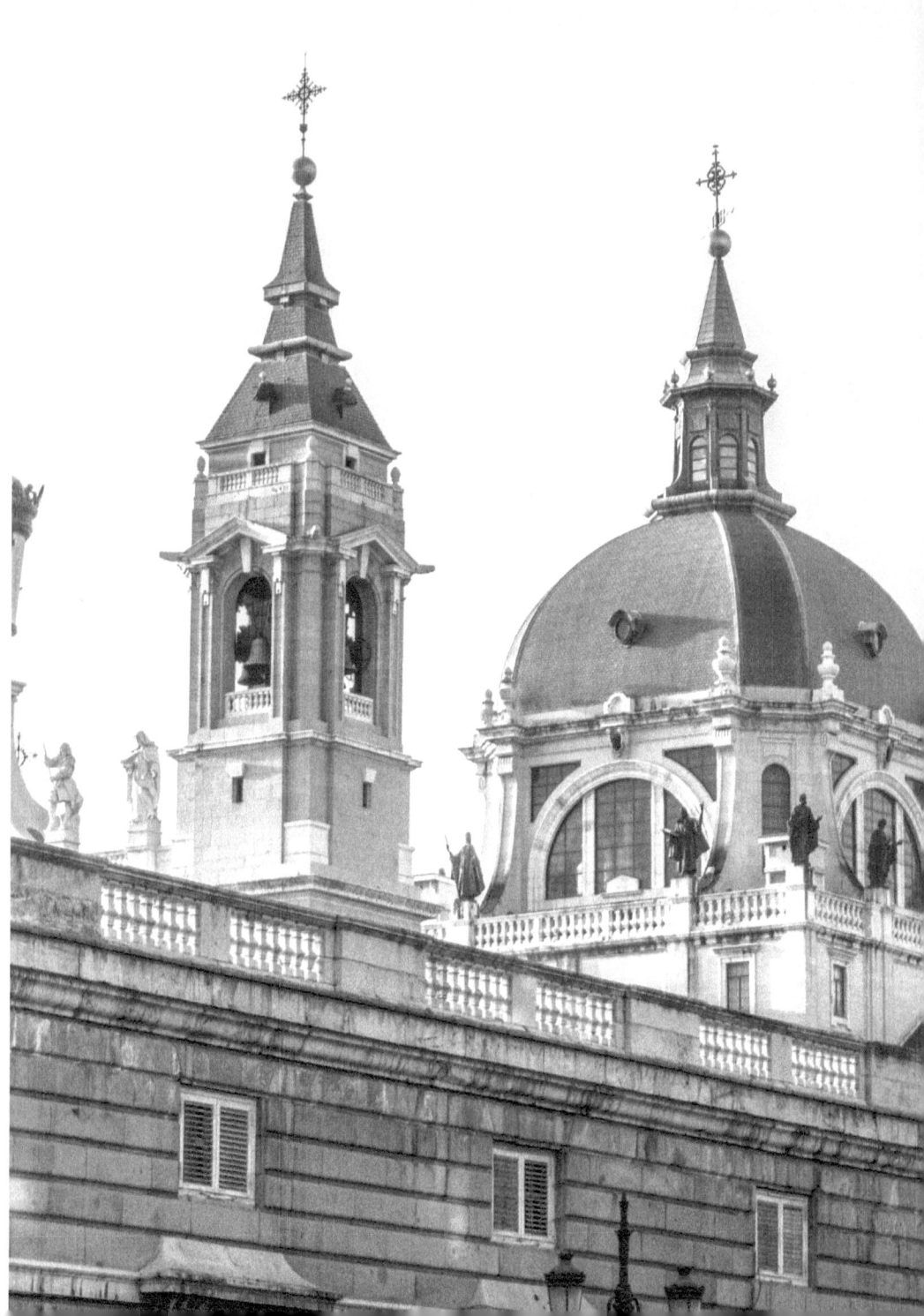

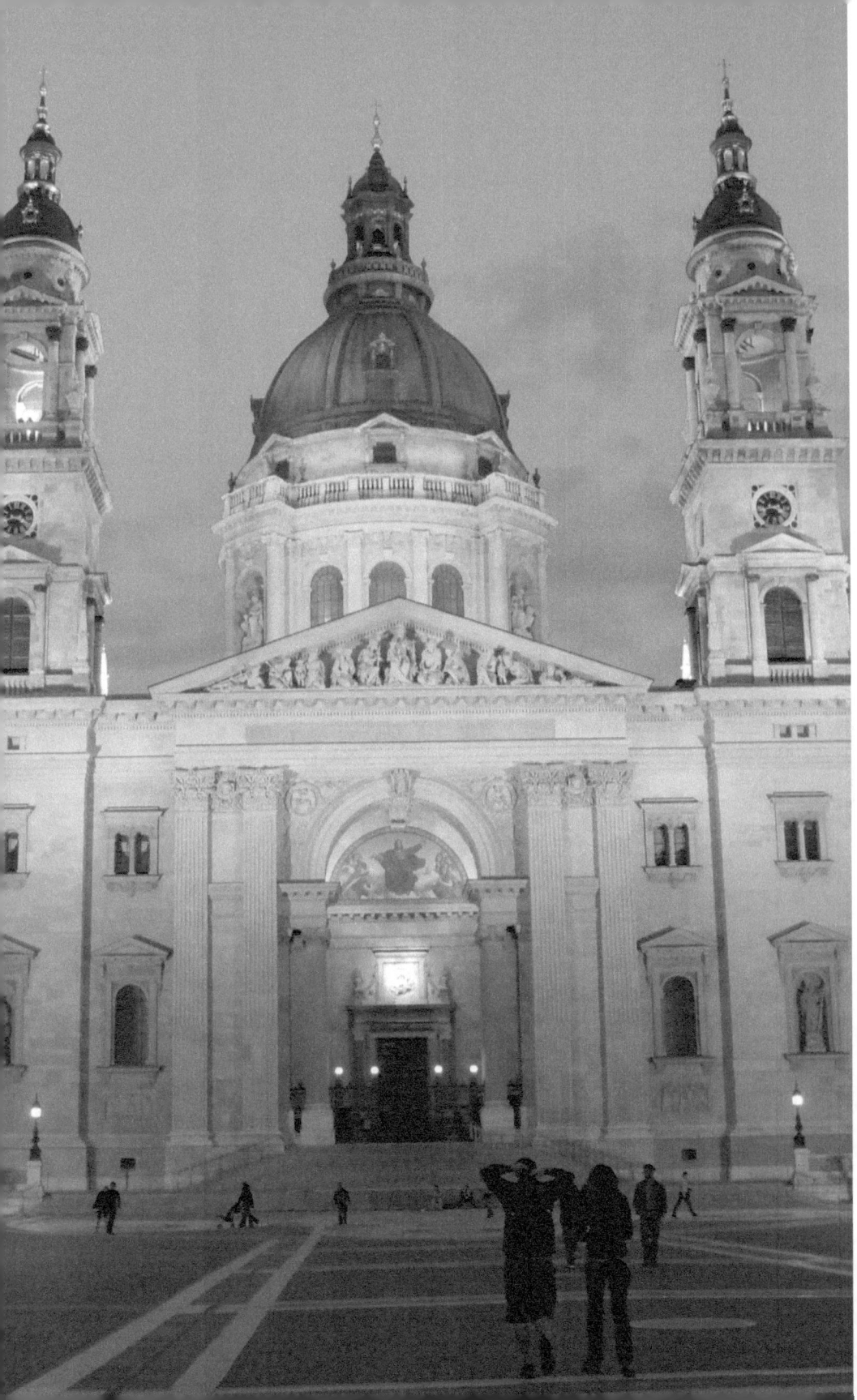

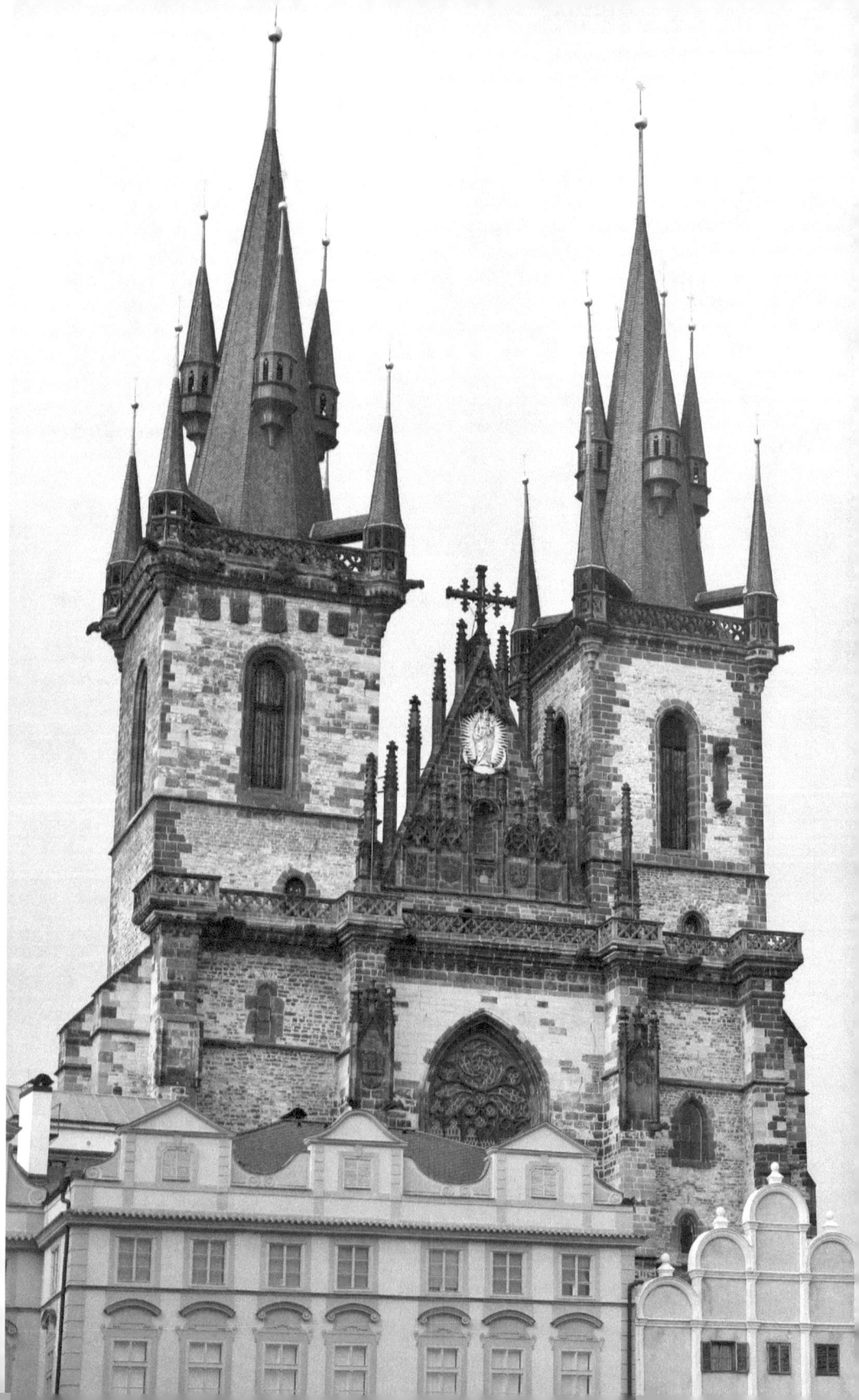

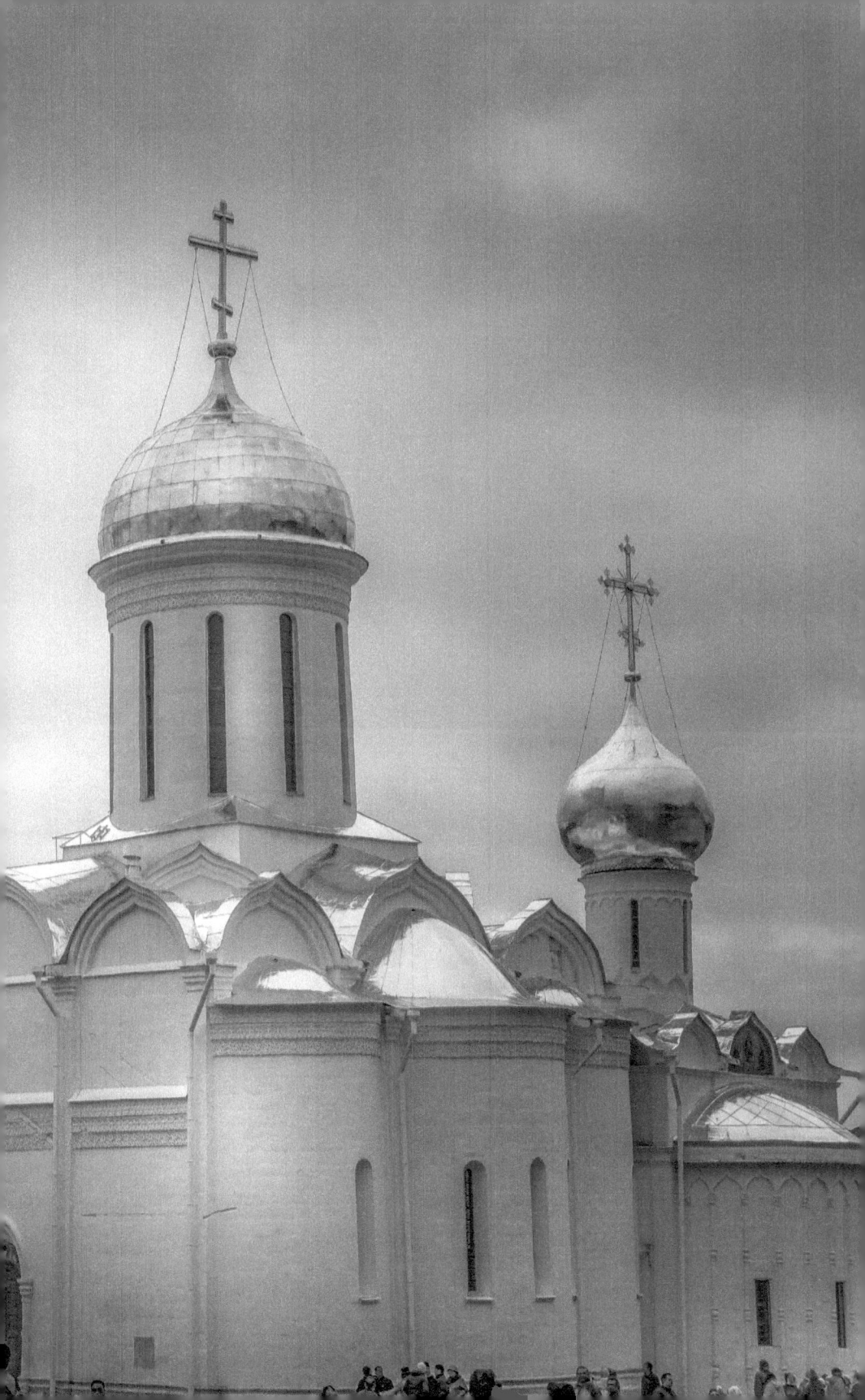

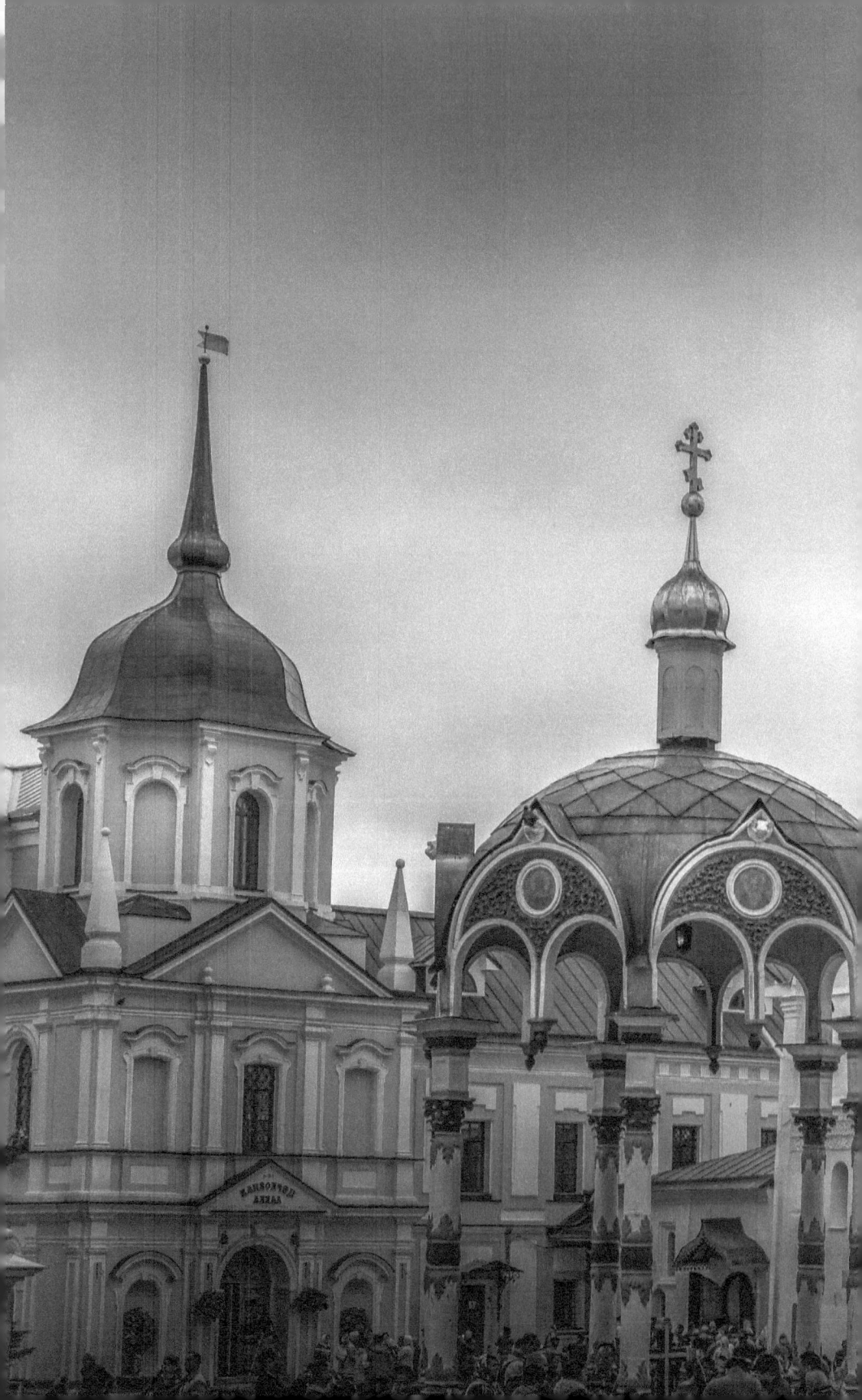

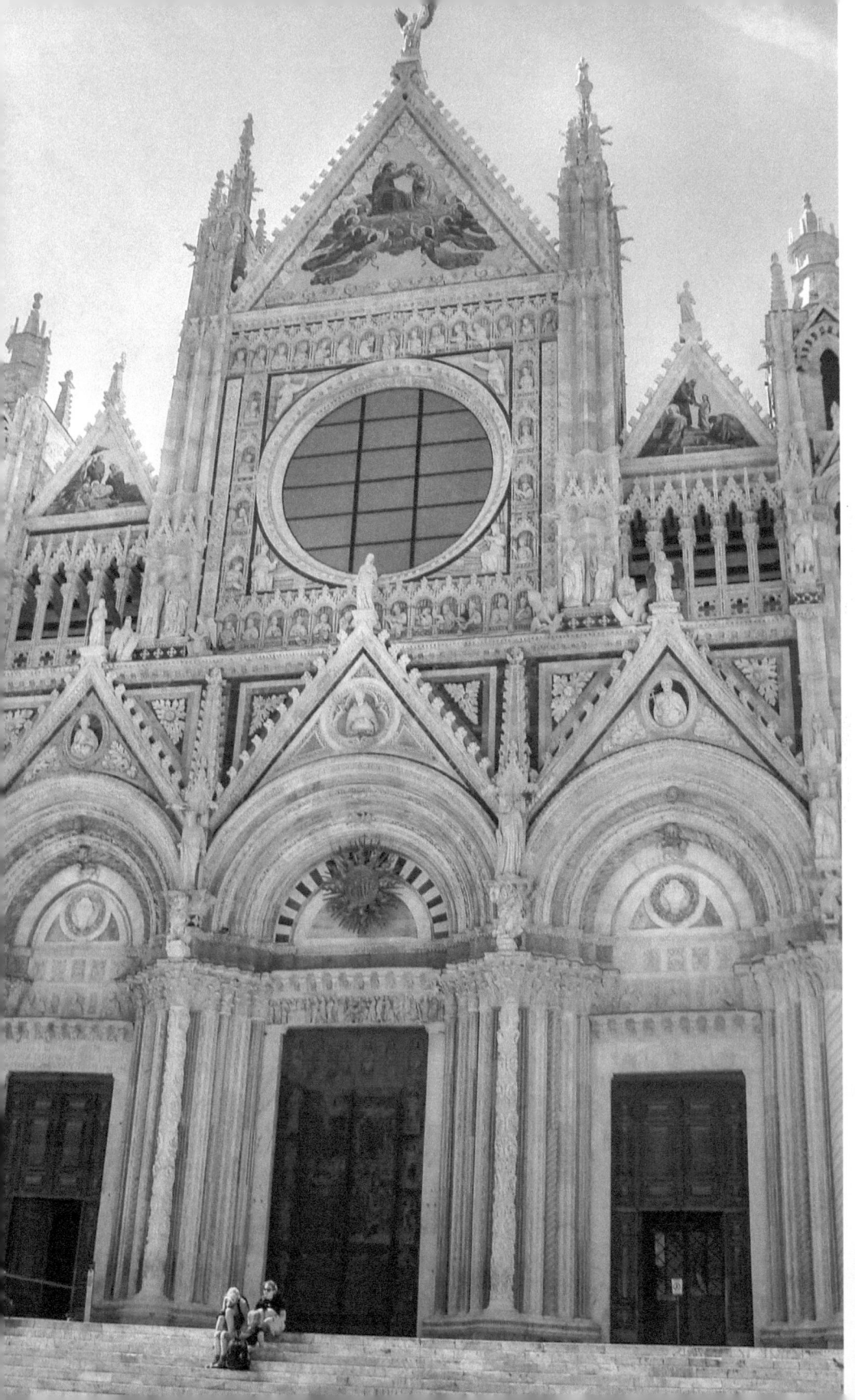

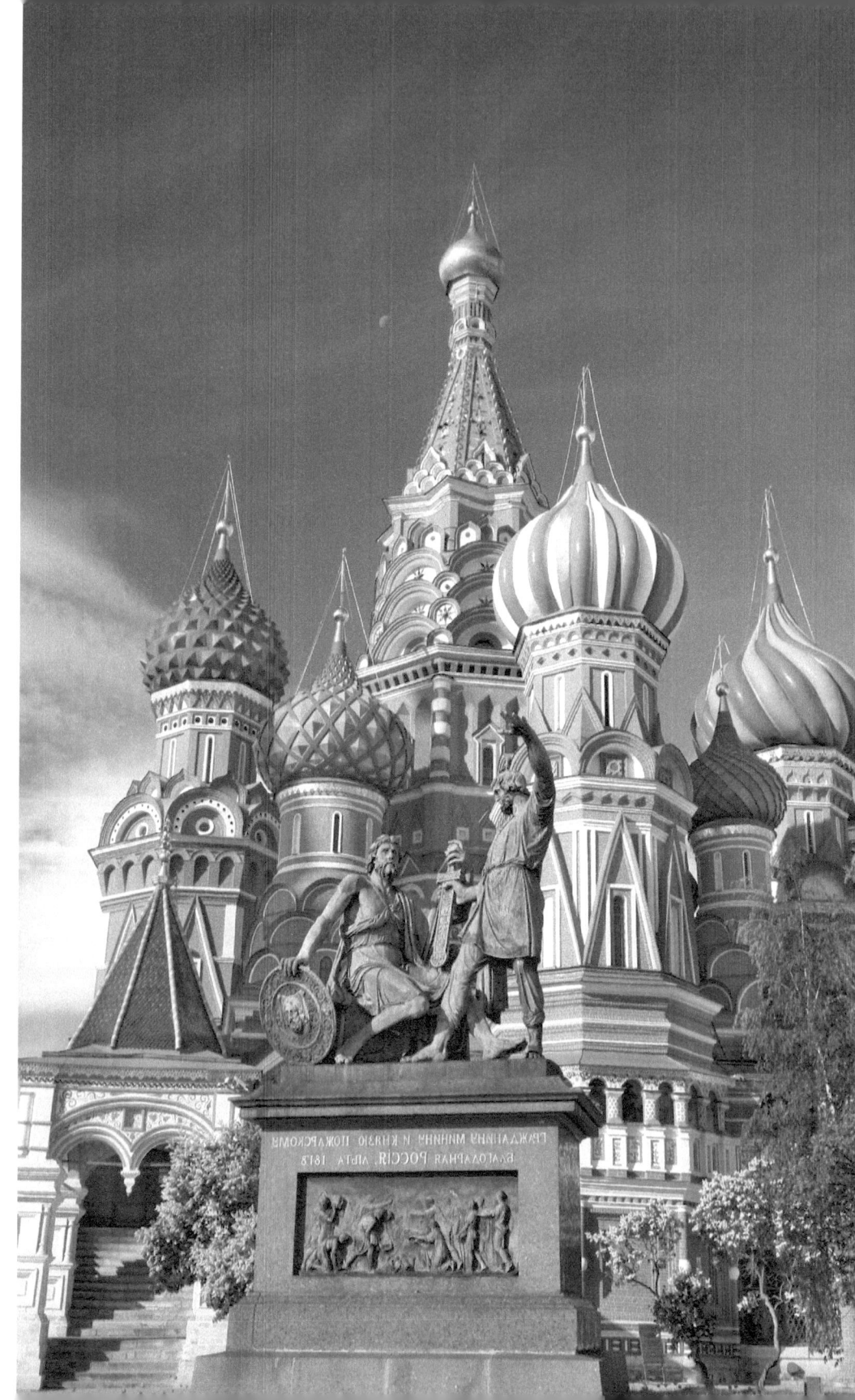

A PHOTO JOURNAL

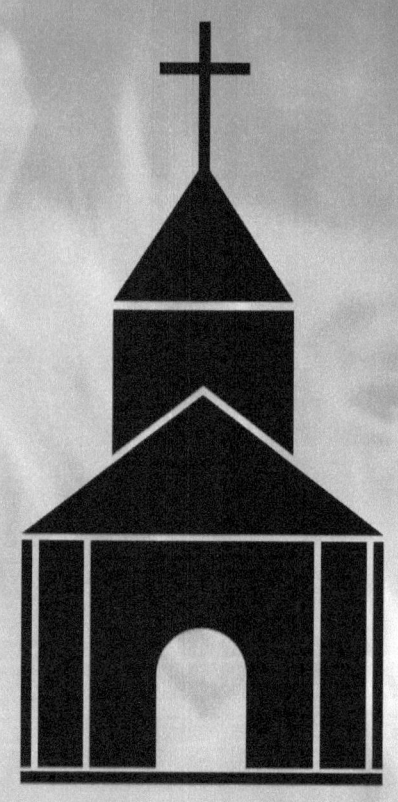

CHURCHES

STEV PETER

www.ingramcontent.com/pod-product-compliance
Lightning Source LLC
Chambersburg PA
CBHW021545200526
45163CB00015B/1921